MAX LUCADO

LIFE LESSONS *from*

PSALMS

A Praise Book for God's People

PREPARED BY THE LIVINGSTONE CORPORATION

Harper*Christian*
Resources

Requests for information should be addressed to:
HarperChristian Resources, 3900 Sparks Dr. SE, Grand Rapids, Michigan 49546

ISBN 978-0-310-08668-0 (softcover)
ISBN 978-0-310-08669-7 (ebook)

CONTENTS

HOW TO STUDY THE BIBLE

The Bible is a peculiar book. Words crafted in another language. Deeds done in a distant era. Events recorded in a far-off land. Counsel offered to a foreign people. It is a peculiar book.

It's surprising that anyone reads it. It's too old. Some of its writings date back 5,000 years. It's too bizarre. The book speaks of incredible floods, fires, earthquakes, and people with supernatural abilities. It's too radical. The Bible calls for undying devotion to a carpenter who called himself God's Son.

Logic says this book shouldn't survive. Too old, too bizarre, too radical.

The Bible has been banned, burned, scoffed, and ridiculed. Scholars have mocked it as foolish. Kings have branded it as illegal. A thousand times over the grave has been dug and the dirge has begun, but somehow the Bible never stays in the grave. Not only has it survived, but it has also thrived. It is the single most popular book in all of history. It has been the bestselling book in the world for years!

There is no way on earth to explain it. Which perhaps is the only explanation. For the Bible's durability is not found on *earth* but in *heaven*. The millions who have tested its claims and claimed its promises know there is but one answer: the Bible is God's book and God's voice.

As you read it, you would be wise to give some thought to two questions: *What is the purpose of the Bible?* and *How do I study the Bible?* Time spent reflecting on these two issues will greatly enhance your Bible study.

What is the purpose of the Bible?

Let the Bible itself answer that question: *"From infancy you have known the Holy Scriptures, which are able to make you wise for salvation through faith in Christ Jesus"* (2 Timothy 3:15).

The purpose of the Bible? Salvation. God's highest passion is to get his children home. His book, the Bible, describes his plan of salvation. The purpose of the Bible is to proclaim God's plan and passion to save his children.

This is the reason why this book has endured through the centuries. It dares to tackle the toughest questions about life: *Where do I go after I die? Is there a God? What do I do with my fears?* The Bible is the treasure map that leads to God's highest treasure—eternal life.

But how do you study the Bible? Countless copies of Scripture sit unread on bookshelves and nightstands simply because people don't know how to read it. What can you do to make the Bible real in your life?

The clearest answer is found in the words of Jesus: *"Ask and it will be given to you; seek and you will find; knock and the door will be opened to you"* (Matthew 7:7).

The first step in understanding the Bible is asking God to help you. You should read it prayerfully. If anyone understands God's Word, it is because of God and not the reader.

"The Advocate, the Holy Spirit, whom the Father will send in my name, will teach you all things and will remind you of everything I have said to you" (John 14:26).

Before reading the Bible, pray and invite God to speak to you. Don't go to Scripture looking for your idea, but go searching for his.

Not only should you read the Bible prayerfully, but you should also read it carefully. *"Seek and you will find"* is the pledge. The Bible is not a newspaper to be skimmed but rather a mine to be quarried. *"If you look for it as for silver and search for it as for hidden treasure, then you will understand the fear of the* Lord *and find the knowledge of God"* (Proverbs 2:4–5).

Any worthy find requires effort. The Bible is no exception. To understand the Bible, you don't have to be brilliant, but you must be willing to roll up your sleeves and search.

"Do your best to present yourself to God as one approved, a worker who does not need to be ashamed and who correctly handles the word of truth" (2 Timothy 2:15).

Here's a practical point. Study the Bible a bit at a time. Hunger is not satisfied by eating twenty-one meals in one sitting once a week. The body needs a steady diet to remain strong. So does the soul. When God sent food to his people in the wilderness, he didn't provide loaves already made. Instead, he sent them manna in the shape of *"thin flakes like frost on the ground"* (Exodus 16:14).

God gave manna in limited portions.

God sends spiritual food the same way. He opens the heavens with just enough nutrients for today's hunger. He provides *"a rule for this, a rule for that; a little here, a little there"* (Isaiah 28:10).

Don't be discouraged if your reading reaps a small harvest. Some days a lesser portion is all that is needed. What is important is to search every day for that day's message. A steady diet of God's Word over a lifetime builds a healthy soul and mind.

It's much like the little girl who returned from her first day at school feeling a bit dejected. Her mom asked, "Did you learn anything?"

"Apparently not enough," the girl responded. "I have to go back tomorrow, and the next day, and the next…"

Such is the case with learning. And such is the case with Bible study. Understanding comes little by little over a lifetime.

There is a third step in understanding the Bible. After the asking and seeking comes the knocking. After you ask and search, *"knock and the door will be opened to you"* (Matthew 7:7).

To knock is to stand at God's door. To make yourself available. To climb the steps, cross the porch, stand at the doorway, and volunteer. Knocking goes beyond the realm of thinking and into the realm of acting.

To knock is to ask, *What can I do? How can I obey? Where can I go?*

It's one thing to know what to do. It's another to do it. But for those who do it—those who choose to obey—a special reward awaits them.

"Whoever looks intently into the perfect law that gives freedom, and continues in it—not forgetting what they have heard, but doing it—they will be blessed in what they do" (James 1:25).

What a promise. Blessings come to those who do what they read in God's Word! It's the same with medicine. If you only read the label but ignore the pills, it won't help. It's the same with food. If you only read the recipe but never cook, you won't be fed. And it's the same with the Bible. If you only read the words but never obey, you'll never know the joy God has promised.

Ask. Search. Knock. Simple, isn't it? So why don't you give it a try? If you do, you'll see why the Bible is the most remarkable book in history.

INTRODUCTION TO
The Book of Psalms

Worship. In two thousand years we haven't worked out the kinks. We still struggle for the right words in prayer. We still fumble over Scripture. We don't know when to kneel. We don't know when to stand. We don't know how to pray.

Worship is a daunting task.

For that reason, God gave us the Psalms—a praise book for God's people. The Psalms could be titled *God's Book of Common Prayer*. This collection of hymns and petitions are strung together by one thread—a heart hungry for God.

Some are defiant. Others are reverent. Some are to be sung. Others are to be prayed. Some are intensely personal. Others are written as if the whole world would use them. Some were penned in caves, others in temples.

But all have one purpose—to give us the words to say when we stand before God.

The very variety should remind us that worship is personal. No secret formula exists. What moves you may stymie another. Each worships differently. But each should worship.

This book will help you do just that.

Here is a hint. Don't just read the prayers of these saints, pray them. Experience their energy. Imitate their honesty. Enjoy their creativity. Let these souls lead you in worship.

And let's remember. The language of worship is not polished, perfect, or advanced. It's just honest.

AUTHOR AND DATE

The book of Psalms consists of 150 individual "psalms" or "hymns" that were written over the span of a century (c. 1440–430 BC) before being compiled into the form we have today sometime during the third century BC. Most of the psalms contain a "superscription" that likely indicates the author (though, in some cases, the name might also refer to a dedication or a collection). King David is listed as the author of 73 psalms, thirteen of which are closely associated with events in his life (3; 7; 18; 34; 51; 52; 54; 56; 57; 59; 60; 63; 142). Asaph, one of David's choirmasters, is the author of twelve psalms (50; 73–83). The sons of Korah, who served in the Temple as musicians, authored ten (42–43; 45–49; 84–85; 87), with one psalm (88) being attributed to Heman the Ezrahite, who was a leading figure in their family. King Solomon composed two psalms (72; 127), and his counselor Ethan the Ezrahite wrote one (89). The oldest psalm (90) was written by Moses. The remaining "orphan" psalms list no author.

SITUATION

The psalms were originally hymns meant to be sung or recited during Temple worship or on other specific occasions. They were often set to music, and many of the superscriptions contain musical notations or instructions on how they were intended to be used in worship. The psalms can generally be divided into several types: (1) *psalms of praise,* which express worship and admiration of God; (2) *psalms of enthronement,* which celebrate God's sovereign rule; (3) *psalms of Zion,* which exalt Mount Zion, God's dwelling place in Jerusalem; (4) *psalms of lament,* in which the author (or nation as a whole) cries out to God for deliverance from distress; (5) *psalms of thanksgiving,* in which the author (or nation) praises God for his acts of deliverance; (6) *psalms of royalty,* which deal with matters relating to earthly kings and the divine kingship of God; (7) *psalms of pilgrimage,* or "songs of ascent," which the Jewish people sang when "going up" to Jerusalem for the annual festivals; (8) *psalms of wisdom,* which uphold the virtues of godliness and proclaim God's rewards for righteous living; (9) *psalms of the law,* which extol the virtues contained in God's law (the Torah); and (10) *psalms of restoration,* which look forward to the future restoration of God's people.

KEY THEMES

- God is worthy of all worship.
- God will defend his people against their enemies.
- Being in relationship with God is the key to all joy and security.

KEY VERSES

I will give thanks to you, Lord, with all my heart; I will tell of all your wonderful deeds (Psalm 9:1).

CONTENTS

THE PATH OF RIGHTEOUSNESS

The LORD knows the way of the righteous,
but the way of the ungodly shall perish.
PSALM 1:6 NKJV

REFLECTION

The phrase "a fork in the road" refers to a crucial time in life where you must make a major decision that you know will impact your future. What are some of these decisions that you have made in your life? How did you ultimately decide what was the correct course to take?

_____

_____

_____

_____

SITUATION

Psalms 1 and 2, composed by an unknown author, serve as a type of prologue or introduction to the entire book of Psalms. The author invites his readers to take delight in the Lord, follow his ways, and continually strive to have a pure heart before him. Leading such a life leads to fruitfulness, joy, and blessings from God. But the way of the wicked leads to another end: futility, sorrow, and judgment. The author's message is clear: seek the path of righteousness!

OBSERVATION

*Read Psalm 1:1–6 from the New International
Version or the New King James Version.*

NEW INTERNATIONAL VERSION

[1] Blessed is the one
    who does not walk in step with the wicked
or stand in the way that sinners take
    or sit in the company of mockers,
[2] but whose delight is in the law of the LORD,

and who meditates on his law day and night.
³ That person is like a tree planted by streams of water,
    which yields its fruit in season
and whose leaf does not wither—
    whatever they do prospers.

⁴ Not so the wicked!
    They are like chaff
    that the wind blows away.
⁵ Therefore the wicked will not stand in the judgment,
    nor sinners in the assembly of the righteous.
⁶ For the LORD watches over the way of the righteous,
    but the way of the wicked leads to destruction.

NEW KING JAMES VERSION
¹ Blessed is the man
Who walks not in the counsel of the ungodly,
Nor stands in the path of sinners,
Nor sits in the seat of the scornful;
² But his delight is in the law of the LORD,
And in His law he meditates day and night.
³ He shall be like a tree
Planted by the rivers of water,
That brings forth its fruit in its season,
Whose leaf also shall not wither;
And whatever he does shall prosper.

⁴ The ungodly are not so,
But are like the chaff which the wind drives away.
⁵ Therefore the ungodly shall not stand in the judgment,
Nor sinners in the congregation of the righteous.
⁶ For the LORD knows the way of the righteous,
But the way of the ungodly shall perish.

EXPLORATION

1. What is the difference between a good person and a wicked person?

_____

_____

_____

_____

2. What does it mean to "delight" in the law of the Lord?

_____

_____

_____

_____

_____

3. How can righteous people remain pure?

_____

_____

_____

_____

4. What are the kinds of fruit that God's people produce?

_____

_____

_____

_____

5. What future awaits unrighteous people?

_____

_____

_____

_____

6. What are the end results of righteous living and selfish living?

_____

_____

_____

INSPIRATION

Jesus once said, "A good man brings good things out of the good stored up in his heart, and an evil man brings evil things out of the evil stored up in his heart. For the mouth speaks what the heart is full of" (Luke 6:45). . . .

The heart is the center of the spiritual life. If the fruit of a tree is bad, you don't try to fix the fruit; you treat the roots. And if a person's actions are evil, it's not enough to change habits; you have to go deeper. You have to go to the heart of the problem, which is the problem of the heart. That is why the state of the heart is so critical. What is the state of yours?

When someone barks at you, do you bark back or bite your tongue? That depends on the state of your heart.

When your schedule is too tight or your to-do list too long, do you lose your cool or keep it? That depends on the state of your heart.

When you are offered a morsel of gossip marinated in slander, do you turn it down or pass it on? That depends on the state of your heart.

Do you see the bag lady on the street as a burden on society or as an opportunity for God? That, too, depends on the state of your heart.

The state of your heart dictates whether you harbor a grudge or give grace, seek self-pity or seek Christ, drink human misery or taste God's mercy. No wonder, then, the wise man begs, "Above all else, guard your heart" (Proverbs 4:23).

David's prayer should be ours: "Create in me a pure heart, O God" (Psalm 51:10).

And Jesus' statement rings true: "Blessed are the pure in heart, for they will see God" (Matthew 5:8).

Note the order of this beatitude: first purify the heart, then you will see God. Clean the refinery, and the result will be a pure product. (From *The Applause of Heaven* by Max Lucado.)

REACTION

7. Why is it important for you to guard your heart?

_____

_____

_____

_____

8. How can you evaluate the condition of your heart?

_____

_____

_____

_____

9. How can you protect yourself from evil influences?

_____

_____

_____

_____

10. What habits or actions do you want to work on eliminating from your life?

_____

_____

_____

11. What fruit would you like God to produce in your life?

_____

_____

_____

12. When is it difficult for you to guard your heart?

_____

_____

_____

LIFE LESSONS

Psalm 1 presents us with two paths that we can take in life. We can take the way of the righteous, or we can go the way of the wicked. Righteous people are blessed, God-centered, Word-saturated, grounded, and prosperous. The wicked are empty, wind-blown, and vulnerable to judgment. The way of the righteous is lived under God's watchful care. The other way is self-centered and self-directed. Jesus also spoke of only two ways to go through life. We can either go through the "narrow gate," which leads to life, or through the "broad gate," which leads to destruction (see Matthew 7:13–14). The simplicity of the two ways compels each of us to make the crucial choice: _which way will we choose?_ Will we follow our own agenda, or will we completely and wholeheartedly submit to Christ? Two paths . . . but only one choice.

DEVOTION

Father, we know that selfishness doesn't belong in our hearts. May your Word enlighten us and lead us to the path of righteousness. Open our eyes to our weaknesses and give us the courage to change what needs to be changed. Help us to bear lasting fruit for your kingdom.

JOURNALING

In what area of your life do you need to more completely pursue God's path of righteousness?

_____

_____

_____

_____

_____

_____

_____

_____

_____

_____

_____

_____

_____

_____

_____

_____

_____

_____

FOR FURTHER READING

To complete the book of Psalms during this twelve-part study, read Psalms 1–14. For more Bible passages about righteousness, read Proverbs 11:18; Hosea 10:12; Matthew 5:6; Romans 1:17; 2 Corinthians 5:21; Philippians 1:9–11; 1 Timothy 6:11; and James 3:17–18.

COMFORT AND REST

Even though I walk through the darkest valley,
I will fear no evil, for you are with me; your
rod and your staff, they comfort me.
PSALM 23:4

REFLECTION

Think of a time when you felt lonely or discouraged—when you were walking through an especially "dark valley" in life. Where did you turn for help? What was the outcome?

_____

_____

_____

_____

_____

SITUATION

Psalm 23, believed to have been written by King David, is one of the best-known and most-loved of all the psalms in the Bible. Part of its appeal can be attributed to the way in which David depicts God—as a loving shepherd who guides his flock through dangerous valleys and leads them to quiet and peaceful streams. Jesus would later draw on this same imagery to describe himself as the "good shepherd [who] lays down his life for the sheep" (John 10:11). David also pictures God as a host of a banquet who sets out a feast in "the presence of [his] enemies" (Psalm 23:5). In the presence of God, we can always find comfort, peace, and rest, even when we are surrounding by the greatest toils and stresses of life.

OBSERVATION

Read Psalm 23:1–6 from the New International
Version or the New King James Version.

NEW INTERNATIONAL VERSION
¹ The LORD is my shepherd, I lack nothing.
    ² He makes me lie down in green pastures,

he leads me beside quiet waters,
    [3] he refreshes my soul.
He guides me along the right paths
    for his name's sake.
[4] Even though I walk
    through the darkest valley,
I will fear no evil,
    for you are with me;
your rod and your staff,
    they comfort me.

[5] You prepare a table before me
    in the presence of my enemies.
You anoint my head with oil;
    my cup overflows.
[6] Surely your goodness and love will follow me
    all the days of my life,
and I will dwell in the house of the LORD
    forever.

NEW KING JAMES VERSION
[1] The LORD is my shepherd;
I shall not want.
[2] He makes me to lie down in green pastures;
He leads me beside the still waters.
[3] He restores my soul;
He leads me in the paths of righteousness
For His name's sake.

[4] Yea, though I walk through the valley of the shadow of death,
I will fear no evil;
For You are with me;
Your rod and Your staff, they comfort me.

⁵ You prepare a table before me in the presence of my enemies;
You anoint my head with oil;
My cup runs over.
⁶ Surely goodness and mercy shall follow me
All the days of my life;
And I will dwell in the house of the LORD
Forever.

EXPLORATION

1. In what ways is God like a shepherd?

_____

_____

_____

_____

2. In what ways are we—his followers—all like sheep?

_____

_____

_____

_____

3. How does God care for the needs of his people?

_____

_____

_____

_____

4. What promise are you given for enduring times of hardship and pain?

_____

_____

_____

_____

5. What comes to mind when you think about God preparing a table in the presence of your enemies?

_____

_____

_____

6. What kind of future can God's people expect?

_____

_____

_____

INSPIRATION

It is our weariness that makes the words of the carpenter so compelling. Listen to them: "Come to me, all you who are weary and burdened, and I will give you rest" (Matthew 11:28).

Come to me. The invitation is to come to him. Why him? He offers the invitation as a penniless rabbi in an oppressed nation. He has no political office, no connections with the authorities in Rome. He hasn't written a best-seller or earned a diploma.

Yet, he dares to look into the leathery faces of farmers and tired faces of housewives and offer rest. He looks into the disillusioned eyes of a preacher or two from Jerusalem. He gazes into the cynical stare of a banker and the hungry eyes of a bartender and makes this paradoxical promise: "Take my yoke upon you and learn from me, for I am gentle and humble in heart, and you will find rest for your souls" (verse 29).

The people came. They came out of the cul-de-sacs and office complexes of their day. They brought him the burdens of their existence and he gave them, not religion, not doctrine, not systems, but rest.

As a result, they called him Lord.

As a result, they called him Savior.

Not so much because of what he said, but because of what he did. . . . They all came to Jesus weary with the futility of life. A rejected woman. A confused patriarch. Disoriented disciples. A discouraged missionary.

They all found rest. They found anchor points for their storm-tossed souls. And they found that Jesus was the only man to walk God's earth who claimed to have an answer for man's burdens. "Come to me," he invited them.

My prayer is that you, too, will find rest. And that you will sleep like a baby. (From *Six Hours One Friday* by Max Lucado.)

REACTION

7. How is Jesus' offer of rest relevant to you today?

_____

_____

_____

_____

8. In what ways have you already experienced God's rest?

_____

_____

_____

_____

9. What keeps people from fully enjoying the rest that God provides?

_____

_____

_____

_____

10. How have you recently experienced God's comfort and rest?

_____

_____

_____

_____

11. David thought of God as his shepherd. What picture or comparison describes your relationship with God? Why that image?

_____

_____

_____

_____

_____

12. In what area of your life do you need God's guidance and rest for your soul?

_____

_____

_____

_____

LIFE LESSONS

David wrote, "The LORD . . . makes me lie down in green pastures" (Psalm 23:1–2). Sometimes, we don't know when to stop the pace of our busy lives. And, more seriously, we don't know *how* to stop. But, as David tells us, our watchful Shepherd knows just how desperately at times we need to just rest. Our Lord wants us to develop a personal rhythm between work and rest. Too many people are "burning the candle at both ends" and "running on empty." There is no honor in working ourselves to death! Jesus himself knew just how important rest was for his own life and for his disciples. He said to them, "Come with me by yourselves to a quiet place and get some rest" (Mark 6:31). Jesus, our Good Shepherd, extends the same offer to us today. We just need to allow him to lead us out of our hectic and stressful times and into his rest.

DEVOTION

Father, you are God and Creator, but we come to you as lost sheep in need of a shepherd. We need you to hold us, comfort us, and give us the rest that only you can provide. Thank you for your offer of peace for our souls. Heal our wounds and give us new strength to follow you.

JOURNALING

What do you need to put aside today so you can enter God's presence and receive his rest?

_____

_____

_____

_____

_____

_____

_____

_____

_____

_____

_____

_____

FOR FURTHER READING

To complete the book of Psalms during this twelve-part study, read Psalms 15–26. For more Bible passages about finding comfort and rest, read Exodus 33:12–14; Psalm 62:1; Isaiah 49:13; Jeremiah 6:16; 31:13; Matthew 11:28–30; 2 Corinthians 1:3–4; and Hebrews 4:1–11.

CONFESSING OUR SINS

I acknowledged my sin to You, and my iniquity
I have not hidden. I said, "I will confess
my transgressions to the LORD," and
You forgave the iniquity of my sin.
PSALM 32:5 NKJV

REFLECTION

Think of a time when you received forgiveness from a friend. How did it make you feel?

_____

_____

_____

_____

_____

SITUATION

It is not known when David penned Psalm 32 or the situation that gave rise to his words. However, the Bible records several instances when David sinned before God . . . and suffered the consequences for his actions. On one occasion, he committed adultery with Bathsheba and arranged for her husband to be killed in battle. As a result, the child born through their illicit union died (see 2 Samuel 11–12). Another time, David conducted a census of the people against God's will, with the consequence that 70,000 people died in a plague (see 2 Samuel 24). David well understood the damage that sin can cause—and the blessings we receive when we confess those sins to God and receive his grace and forgiveness.

OBSERVATION

Read Psalm 32:1–11 from the New International
Version or the New King James Version.

NEW INTERNATIONAL VERSION
[1] Blessed is the one
    whose transgressions are forgiven,
    whose sins are covered.

[2] Blessed is the one
  whose sin the LORD does not count against them
  and in whose spirit is no deceit.

[3] When I kept silent,
  my bones wasted away
  through my groaning all day long.
[4] For day and night
  your hand was heavy on me;
my strength was sapped
  as in the heat of summer.

[5] Then I acknowledged my sin to you
  and did not cover up my iniquity.
I said, "I will confess
  my transgressions to the LORD."
And you forgave
  the guilt of my sin.

[6] Therefore let all the faithful pray to you
  while you may be found;
surely the rising of the mighty waters
  will not reach them.
[7] You are my hiding place;
  you will protect me from trouble
  and surround me with songs of deliverance.

[8] I will instruct you and teach you in the way you should go;
  I will counsel you with my loving eye on you.
[9] Do not be like the horse or the mule,
  which have no understanding
but must be controlled by bit and bridle
  or they will not come to you.

¹⁰ Many are the woes of the wicked,
    but the LORD's unfailing love
    surrounds the one who trusts in him.

¹¹ Rejoice in the LORD and be glad, you righteous;
    sing, all you who are upright in heart!

NEW KING JAMES VERSION
¹ Blessed is he whose transgression is forgiven,
Whose sin is covered.
² Blessed is the man to whom the LORD does not impute iniquity,
And in whose spirit there is no deceit.

³ When I kept silent, my bones grew old
Through my groaning all the day long.
⁴ For day and night Your hand was heavy upon me;
My vitality was turned into the drought of summer. Selah
⁵ I acknowledged my sin to You,
And my iniquity I have not hidden.
I said, "I will confess my transgressions to the LORD,"
And You forgave the iniquity of my sin. Selah

⁶ For this cause everyone who is godly shall pray to You
In a time when You may be found;
Surely in a flood of great waters
They shall not come near him.
⁷ You are my hiding place;
You shall preserve me from trouble;
You shall surround me with songs of deliverance. Selah

⁸ I will instruct you and teach you in the way you should go;
I will guide you with My eye.
⁹ Do not be like the horse or like the mule,

Which have no understanding,
Which must be harnessed with bit and bridle,
Else they will not come near you.
[10] Many sorrows shall be to the wicked;
But he who trusts in the LORD, mercy shall surround him.
[11] Be glad in the LORD and rejoice, you righteous;
And shout for joy, all you upright in heart!

EXPLORATION

1. How does David describe what it was like when he "kept silent" and did not confess his sin?

_____

_____

_____

_____

_____

2. Why do you think people try to hide their sins from God?

_____

_____

_____

_____

_____

3. What happens when people refuse to confess their wrongdoing to God?

_____

_____

_____

_____

_____

4. How can people find relief from the shame and guilt of sin?

_____

_____

_____

_____

_____

5. What promises are you given when you confess your sin and repent?

_____

_____

_____

_____

_____

6. How does God want people to react to his correction?

_____

_____

_____

_____

_____

INSPIRATION

Oh, the hands of Jesus. Hands of incarnation at his birth. Hands of liberation as he healed. Hands of inspiration as he taught. Hands of dedication as he served. And hands of salvation as he died.

The crowd at the cross concluded that the purpose of the pounding was to skewer the hands of Christ to a beam. But they were only half-right. We can't fault them for missing the other half. They couldn't see it. But Jesus could. And heaven could. And we can.

Through the eyes of Scripture we see what others missed but what Jesus saw. "[He] canceled the charge of our legal indebtedness, which stood against us and condemned us; he has taken it away, nailing it to the cross" (Colossians 2:14).

Between his hand and the wood there was a list. A long list. A list of our mistakes: our lusts and lies and greedy moments and prodigal years. A list of our sins.

Dangling from the cross is an itemized catalog of your sins. The bad decisions from last year. The bad attitudes from last week. There, in broad daylight for all of heaven to see, is a list of your mistakes.

God has penned a list of our faults. The list God has made, however, cannot be read. The words can't be deciphered. The mistakes are covered. The sins are hidden. Those at the top are hidden by his hand; those down the list are covered by his blood. Your sins are blotted out by Jesus. "God brought you alive—right along with Christ! Think of it! All sins forgiven, the slate wiped clean, that old arrest warrant canceled and nailed to Christ's cross" (Colossians 2:13–14 MSG)....

What kept Jesus from resisting? This warrant, this tabulation of your failures. He knew the price of those sins was death. He knew the source of those sins was you, and since he couldn't bear the thought of eternity without you, he chose the nails. (From *He Chose the Nails* by Max Lucado.)

REACTION

7. How do you respond to the idea that when you confess and repent of your sin, those mistakes are "hidden" in God's sight? In what ways is that hard for you to believe?

_____

_____

_____

_____

8. What are some factors that keep people from seeking God's forgiveness? What tends to keep people from receiving his forgiveness?

_____

_____

_____

_____

_____

9. When is a time that you experienced God's forgiveness?

_____

_____

_____

_____

_____

10. How should the fact you are forgiven affect your relationships with others?

_____

_____

_____

_____

_____

11. How are you acknowledging that Jesus is truly the Lord of your life?

_____

_____

_____

_____

_____

12. In what ways can you express your joy and appreciation to God for his forgiveness?

_____

_____

_____

_____

_____

_____

LIFE LESSONS

The path to the blessings of forgiveness begins with the first step of honest confession. Jesus declared that he had come into the world to save sinners who need forgiveness—not the self-righteous who refuse to admit their need for him. "I have not come to call the righteous, but sinners" (Mark 2:17). To refuse to admit we have sin is to refuse God's cleansing grace! Even more, as David points out in Psalm 32:3, unconfessed sin makes us unhealthy as well as unholy. Paul pointed out that many believers in the Corinthian church were weak and sick because they sinfully misused the Lord's Table (see 1 Corinthians 11:30–31). Confession of sin, on the other hand, honors God and the love he showed in sending Jesus as the sacrifice for sin. In view of the cross, God holds nothing against us, and he longs to be in a loving, caring, guiding, protecting relationship with us. Confession moves us through the door of God's amazing grace.

DEVOTION

Father, you know us early in the morning; you know us late at night. You know us when we're weak; you know us when we're strong. Help us when we try to hide our sins from you. Father, forgive us and transform us into your likeness. Remind us that you will always love us.

JOURNALING

What sins do you need to confess today to God?

_____

_____

_____

_____

_____

_____

_____

_____

_____

_____

_____

_____

_____

_____

_____

_____

_____

_____

_____

FOR FURTHER READING

To complete the book of Psalms during this twelve-part study, read Psalms 27–39. For more Bible passages about forgiveness, read Psalm 130:4; Matthew 6:12–15; 26:26–29; Luke 1:76–79; Acts 5:29–32; Ephesians 1:7–10; Colossians 1:13–14; and 1 John 1:8–10.

RELYING ON GOD'S STRENGTH

God is our refuge and strength,
an ever-present help in trouble.
PSALM 46:1

REFLECTION

What were some of your childhood fears? How did you get over those fears?

_____

_____

_____

_____

_____

_____

SITUATION

The "sons of Korah," the authors of Psalm 46, were the descendants of Moses' cousin Korah. He is best known in the Bible for leading a revolt against Moses, with the result that God sent fire from heaven to consume him and his co-conspirators (see Numbers 16:1–40). His line, however, "did not die out" (26:11), and during the time of David they became the great leaders in choral and orchestral music in the tabernacle. This "psalm of Zion," which was popularized by Martin Luther in his hymn "A Mighty Fortress Is Our God," celebrates the presence of God in all aspects of life—both the good and the bad. It relates how we can always rely on God's strength.

OBSERVATION

Read Psalm 46:1–11 from the New International Version or the New King James Version.

New International Version

[1] God is our refuge and strength,
    an ever-present help in trouble.
[2] Therefore we will not fear, though the earth give way

RELYING ON GOD'S STRENGTH

and the mountains fall into the heart of the sea,
[3] though its waters roar and foam
   and the mountains quake with their surging.

[4] There is a river whose streams make glad the city of God,
   the holy place where the Most High dwells.
[5] God is within her, she will not fall;
   God will help her at break of day.
[6] Nations are in uproar, kingdoms fall;
   he lifts his voice, the earth melts.

[7] The LORD Almighty is with us;
   the God of Jacob is our fortress.

[8] Come and see what the LORD has done,
   the desolations he has brought on the earth.
[9] He makes wars cease
   to the ends of the earth.
He breaks the bow and shatters the spear;
   he burns the shields with fire.
[10] He says, "Be still, and know that I am God;
   I will be exalted among the nations,
   I will be exalted in the earth."

[11] The LORD Almighty is with us;
   the God of Jacob is our fortress.

NEW KING JAMES VERSION
[1] God is our refuge and strength,
A very present help in trouble.
[2] Therefore we will not fear,
Even though the earth be removed,
And though the mountains be carried into the midst of the sea;

³ Though its waters roar and be troubled,
Though the mountains shake with its swelling. Selah

⁴ There is a river whose streams shall make glad the city of God,
The holy place of the tabernacle of the Most High.
⁵ God is in the midst of her, she shall not be moved;
God shall help her, just at the break of dawn.
⁶ The nations raged, the kingdoms were moved;
He uttered His voice, the earth melted.

⁷ The LORD of hosts is with us;
The God of Jacob is our refuge. Selah

⁸ Come, behold the works of the LORD,
Who has made desolations in the earth.
⁹ He makes wars cease to the end of the earth;
He breaks the bow and cuts the spear in two;
He burns the chariot in the fire.

¹⁰ Be still, and know that I am God;
I will be exalted among the nations,
I will be exalted in the earth!

¹¹ The LORD of hosts is with us;
The God of Jacob is our refuge. Selah

EXPLORATION

1. What are some of the calamities the psalmist mentions that cause fear?

_____

_____

_____

_____

2. Why does the psalmist say you do not have to fear anything on earth?

_____

_____

_____

_____

3. How does God protect his people?

_____

_____

_____

_____

4. What are some of the ways the psalmist mentions that God brings peace?

_____

_____

_____

_____

5. How can remembering God's power bring peace to you?

_____

_____

_____

_____

6. Why does God command you to "be still" in times of turmoil and recognize that he is God?

_____

_____

_____

_____

INSPIRATION

When I was ten years old, my mother enrolled me in piano lessons. Now, many youngsters excel at the keyboard. Not me. Spending thirty minutes every afternoon tethered to a piano bench was a torture just one level away from swallowing broken glass. The metronome inspected each second with glacial slowness before it was allowed to pass.

Some of the music, though, I learned to enjoy. I hammered the staccatos. I belabored the crescendos. The thundering finishes I kettle-drummed.

But there was one instruction in the music I could never obey to my teacher's satisfaction. The rest. The zigzagged command to do nothing. Nothing! What sense does that make? Why sit at the piano and pause when you can pound?

"Because," my teacher patiently explained, "music is always sweeter after a rest."

It didn't make sense to me at age ten. But now, a few decades later, the words ring with wisdom—divine wisdom. In fact, the words of my teacher remind me of the convictions of another Teacher.

"Now when Jesus saw the crowds, he went up on a mountainside" (Matthew 5:1). Don't read the sentence so fast you miss the surprise. Matthew didn't write what you would expect him to. The verse doesn't read, "When he saw the crowds, he went into their midst." Or "When he saw the crowds, he healed their hurts." Or "When he saw the crowds, he seated them and began to teach them." On other occasions he did that . . . but not this time.

Before he went to the masses, he went to the mountain. Before the disciples encountered the crowds, they encountered the Christ. And before they faced the people, they were reminded of the sacred. (From *The Applause of Heaven* by Max Lucado.)

REACTION

7. What does Jesus' example say about taking time to be still before God?

_____

_____

_____

_____

_____

8. What happens when you don't take time to be quiet before God?

_____

_____

_____

_____

_____

9. How does spending time in God's presence help you to rely on his strength—not your own?

_____

_____

_____

_____

_____

10. What tends to keep you from spending time with God each day?

_____

_____

_____

_____

11. What are some ways you can overcome these distractions?

_____
_____
_____
_____
_____

12. What advice would you offer a friend who is overwhelmed by fear or anxiety?

_____
_____
_____
_____
_____

LIFE LESSONS

To "be still" does not come naturally to us. Many an exasperated parent, frantically trying to get their kids dressed for church, has exclaimed, "Why can't you just be still!" We're an active people. But there are times that come in life that are too big for us to resolve through our own actions. Times when it seems the earth has given away "and the mountains fall into the heart of the sea" (Psalm 46:2). It is in these moments our heavenly Father beckons, "Be still, and know that I am God" (verse 10). It is only in these moments that we come to experience the wonderful aspects of God's love, care, and power. To be still is not a passive resignation but an active expectancy to witness only what God can do. It is to be still and _watch_ God take charge.

DEVOTION

Father, you have done amazing things. Open our eyes to your power and your wonders. Keep our focus on your greatness rather than on our weakness. Lord, please teach us to be quiet before you. Only as we sit at your feet will our fears be transformed into faith.

JOURNALING

In what ways has God proven to be a mighty fortress of strength in your life?

_____

_____

_____

_____

_____

_____

_____

_____

_____

_____

_____

_____

_____

_____

_____

_____

_____

_____

_____

_____

_____

FOR FURTHER READING

To complete the book of Psalms during this twelve-part study, read Psalms 40–51. For more Bible passages about relying on God's strength, read Exodus 14:13–14; Proverbs 3:5; Isaiah 26:4–6; Jeremiah 17:5–9; Zechariah 4:1–6; Matthew 11:28–30; John 15:4–5; and 1 Corinthians 2:1–5.

CONFIDENCE IN GOD

My soul, wait silently for God alone,
for my expectation is from Him.
He only is my rock and my salvation;
He is my defense; I shall not be moved.
PSALM 62:5–6 NKJV

REFLECTION

In what ways is having confidence in your own skills and abilities a good thing? How has having too much confidence in your skills and abilities gotten you into trouble in the past?

_____

_____

_____

_____

SITUATION

The superscription to Psalm 62, which was written by King David, states that this hymn was "for Jeduthun," which likely means this was intended to be sung by his choir. Jeduthun is mentioned in the Bible as being "responsible for the sounding of the trumpets and cymbals and for the playing of the other instruments for sacred song" (1 Chronicles 16:42). The setting of this psalm of David arises out of a context of adversity (possibly the rebellion of his son Absalom), but throughout David expresses his complete confidence in God's ability to deliver him. David's words reveal that when we are facing trials at the hands of others, we can always place our confidence in God and look to him to give us rest for our weary souls.

OBSERVATION

Read Psalm 62:1–12 from the New International
Version or the New King James Version.

NEW INTERNATIONAL VERSION
¹ Truly my soul finds rest in God;
my salvation comes from him.

² Truly he is my rock and my salvation;
  he is my fortress, I will never be shaken.

³ How long will you assault me?
  Would all of you throw me down—
  this leaning wall, this tottering fence?
⁴ Surely they intend to topple me
  from my lofty place;
  they take delight in lies.
With their mouths they bless,
  but in their hearts they curse.

⁵ Yes, my soul, find rest in God;
  my hope comes from him.
⁶ Truly he is my rock and my salvation;
  he is my fortress, I will not be shaken.
⁷ My salvation and my honor depend on God;
  he is my mighty rock, my refuge.
⁸ Trust in him at all times, you people;
  pour out your hearts to him,
  for God is our refuge.

⁹ Surely the lowborn are but a breath,
  the highborn are but a lie.
If weighed on a balance, they are nothing;
  together they are only a breath.
¹⁰ Do not trust in extortion
  or put vain hope in stolen goods;
though your riches increase,
  do not set your heart on them.

¹¹ One thing God has spoken,
  two things I have heard:

"Power belongs to you, God,
    [12] and with you, Lord, is unfailing love";
and, "You reward everyone
    according to what they have done."

NEW KING JAMES VERSION
[1] Truly my soul silently waits for God;
From Him comes my salvation.
[2] He only is my rock and my salvation;
He is my defense;
I shall not be greatly moved.

[3] How long will you attack a man?
You shall be slain, all of you,
Like a leaning wall and a tottering fence.
[4] They only consult to cast him down from his high position;
They delight in lies;
They bless with their mouth,
But they curse inwardly. Selah

[5] My soul, wait silently for God alone,
For my expectation is from Him.
[6] He only is my rock and my salvation;
He is my defense;
I shall not be moved.
[7] In God is my salvation and my glory;
The rock of my strength,
And my refuge, is in God.

[8] Trust in Him at all times, you people;
Pour out your heart before Him;
God is a refuge for us. Selah

[9] Surely men of low degree are a vapor,
Men of high degree are a lie;
If they are weighed on the scales,
They are altogether lighter than vapor.
[10] Do not trust in oppression,
Nor vainly hope in robbery;
If riches increase,
Do not set your heart on them.

[11] God has spoken once,
Twice I have heard this:
That power belongs to God.
[12] Also to You, O Lord, belongs mercy;
For You render to each one according to his work.

EXPLORATION

1. What are some of the images that David uses to show his confidence in God?

_____

_____

_____

2. Who is David addressing in verse 3? What do these individuals try to do?

_____

_____

_____

3. What is David's response to the threats that come in life?

_____

_____

4. How does this psalm encourage you to likewise deal with problems and pain?

_____

_____

_____

5. What does this passage reveal about the value of power, wealth, and status?

_____

_____

_____

6. What are some the ways you have seen God reward his people?

_____

_____

_____

INSPIRATION

It's the expression of Jesus that puzzles us. We've never seen his face like this.

Jesus smiling, yes.

Jesus weeping, absolutely.

Jesus stern, even that.

But Jesus anguished? Cheeks streaked with tears? Face flooded in sweat? Rivulets of blood dripping from his chin? You remember the night.

Jesus knelt down and prayed, saying, "'Father, if it is Your will, take this cup away from Me; nevertheless not My will, but Yours, be done.' . . . His sweat became like great drops of blood falling down to the ground" (Luke 22:42, 44 NKJV).

Jesus was more than anxious; he was afraid. How remarkable that Jesus felt such fear. But how kind that he told us about it. We tend to do the opposite. Gloss over our fears. Cover them up. Keep our sweaty palms in our pockets, our nausea and dry mouths a secret. Not so with Jesus. We see no mask of strength. But we do hear a request for strength.

"Father, if you are willing, take away this cup of suffering." The first one to hear his fear is his Father. He could have gone to his mother. He could have confided in his disciples. He could have assembled a prayer meeting.

All would have been appropriate, but none was his priority.

How did Jesus endure the terror of the crucifixion? He went first to the Father with his fears. He modeled the words of Psalm 62:5: "Yes, my soul, find rest in God; my hope comes from him." Do the same with your fears. Don't avoid life's Gardens of Gethsemane. Enter them. Just don't enter them alone.

And while there, be honest. Pounding the ground is permitted. Tears are allowed. And if you sweat blood, you won't be the first. Do what Jesus did; open your heart. (From *3:16—The Numbers of Hope* by Max Lucado.)

REACTION

7. How did Jesus respond to the fear he experienced in the Garden of Gethsemane?

_____

_____

_____

_____

8. How did Jesus' prayer demonstrate that he had complete confidence in God's plans?

_____

_____

_____

_____

9. What are some "Gardens of Gethsemane" that you have been avoiding?

_____

_____

_____

_____

10. What does Jesus' example reveal about how to face your fears?

_____

_____

_____

_____

11. How has your confidence in God helped you face life's challenges?

_____

_____

_____

_____

12. What steps can you take to continue to trust God in every situation?

_____

_____

_____

_____

LIFE LESSONS

David in this psalm declares two seemingly opposing truths about God. On the one hand, God is a "mighty rock" and all-powerful (Psalm 62:7). On the other hand, God has "unfailing love" for his people (verse 12). A God who is only powerful can seem scary and unapproachable. A God who is only loving can seem limp and ineffective. But when the two are combined—strength *and* love—we can have complete confidence that he not only has the ability to save us from our trials but also cares enough about us to act. In fact, he cares so much that he sent his only Son to save us from our sins. He alone can make us new—forgiven and empowered by his Holy Spirit to live new lives. In turn, we are invited to "be imitators of God" (Ephesians 5:1 NKJV) and offer hope and help to those who have also lost their way.

DEVOTION

Lord, the trials that come our way can cause us to doubt that you have the power and the concern to help us in our times of need. Help us to remember the promises in your Word and never doubt your love for us. We place our confidence completely in you today.

JOURNALING

How will you continue to demonstrate your unfailing trust in God alone?

FOR FURTHER READING

To complete the book of Psalms during this twelve-part study, read Psalms 52–64. For more Bible passages about confidence in God's power, read Exodus 15:1–3; Proverbs 14:26; 18:10; 30:5; Isaiah 25:1–5; Jeremiah 16:19–21; Joel 3:16; Nahum 1:7–8; Habakkuk 3:17–19; 2 Thessalonians 3:2–4; and Ephesians 6:10–20.

LESSON SIX

TRUSTING IN GOD'S GOODNESS

My flesh and my heart may fail, but God is the strength of my heart and my portion forever.

Psalm 73:26

REFLECTION

Think of someone you know who has relied on God for help during a difficult time. How does that example encourage you? How has it demonstrated God's goodness to you?

_____

_____

_____

_____

_____

SITUATION

Asaph, the author of Psalm 73, was one of three musicians (along with Heman and Jeduthun) whom David commissioned to be in charge of singing in the Temple. He also was credited with performing at the dedication of Solomon's Temple (see 2 Chronicles 5:11–14). During Asaph's lengthy tenure, he witnessed suffering among the righteous, while the wicked seemed to prosper. This state of affairs could have led him to despair, but his words in this psalm indicate he had determined to trust in God's goodness and believe his promises. Asaph chose to trust "God is good" (Psalm 73:1) and would deal with "all who are unfaithful" to him (verse 27).

OBSERVATION

Read Psalm 73:21–28 from the New International
Version or the New King James Version.

NEW INTERNATIONAL VERSION
²¹ When my heart was grieved
    and my spirit embittered,

[22] I was senseless and ignorant;
    I was a brute beast before you.

[23] Yet I am always with you;
    you hold me by my right hand.
[24] You guide me with your counsel,
    and afterward you will take me into glory.
[25] Whom have I in heaven but you?
    And earth has nothing I desire besides you.
[26] My flesh and my heart may fail,
    but God is the strength of my heart
    and my portion forever.

[27] Those who are far from you will perish;
    you destroy all who are unfaithful to you.
[28] But as for me, it is good to be near God.
    I have made the Sovereign LORD my refuge;
    I will tell of all your deeds.

NEW KING JAMES VERSION
[21] Thus my heart was grieved,
And I was vexed in my mind.
[22] I was so foolish and ignorant;
I was like a beast before You.
[23] Nevertheless I am continually with You;
You hold me by my right hand.
[24] You will guide me with Your counsel,
And afterward receive me to glory.

[25] Whom have I in heaven but You?
And there is none upon earth that I desire besides You.
[26] My flesh and my heart fail;
But God is the strength of my heart and my portion forever.

²⁷ For indeed, those who are far from You shall perish;
You have destroyed all those who desert You for harlotry.
²⁸ But it is good for me to draw near to God;
I have put my trust in the Lord GOD,
That I may declare all Your works.

EXPLORATION

1. How does Asaph describe the condition of his heart at the beginning of this psalm?

_____

_____

_____

2. What had Asaph learned about God during the course of his life?

_____

_____

_____

3. What kind of future awaits those who trust in God?

_____

_____

_____

4. What are the advantages of living in communion with God?

_____

_____

_____

5. What aspects of God's character does Asaph highlight in this psalm?

_____

_____

_____

6. Why is it important to just let God deal with the wicked and the unjust?

_____

_____

_____

INSPIRATION

I really want to find that verse in the Bible that promises no persecution and violence for Christians. I want to find that verse that promises an easy and pain-free life for the righteous. I want to claim it and hold it up to God so Christians will never suffer for their faith again.

Unfortunately, I can't find it. I find just the opposite. Hebrews 11, the Bible's brief biography of God's best of the best, is difficult to read: "Others were tortured, not accepting deliverance, that they might obtain a better resurrection. Still others had trial of mockings and scourgings, yes, and of chains and imprisonment. They were stoned, they were sawn in two, were tempted, were slain with the sword. They wandered about in sheepskins and goatskins, being destitute, afflicted, tormented" (verses 35–37 NKJV). This is how God treats his friends.

Jesus sent out the Twelve for an Israel-wide revival, promising healings and miracles for everyone—oh, and persecution. In Matthew 10, Jesus, in one of the most discouraging "Win One for the Gipper" speeches, said, "Be on your guard; you will be handed over to the local councils and be flogged in the synagogues . . . when they arrest you . . . put [you] to death . . . you will be hated by everyone . . . [but] when you are persecuted . . . do not be afraid of those who kill the body but cannot kill the soul" (verses 17, 19, 21–23, 28).

Thanks, Jesus. Can't wait.

Some of those friends liked persecution. Like Paul: "That is why, for Christ's sake, I delight in weaknesses, in insults, in hardships, in persecutions, in difficulties. For when I am weak, then I am strong" (2 Corinthians 12:10). Paul thought it built character. Maybe he was right.

Persecution and suffering is inevitable. Even Jesus couldn't escape it. In fact, he became the poster child for persecution, the rallying cry of others who would die for their faith. Revelation speaks of martyred souls crying out for justice now and in the future (see 6:9–11).

Persecution is necessary for the advancement of the gospel. The death of Stephen in Acts 7 caused the gospel to spread to distant lands. In China, where the persecution of Christians was high, the church exploded in growth as those outside the faith saw believers sacrificing their lives and their bodies.

In Romans 8:35, Paul asks, "Who shall separate us from the love of Christ? Shall trouble or hardship or persecution or famine or nakedness or danger or sword?" He answers his own question with this response: "For I am persuaded that neither death nor life, nor angels nor principalities nor powers, nor things present nor things to come, nor height nor depth, nor any other created thing, shall be able to separate us from the love of God which is in Christ Jesus our Lord" (verses 38–39 NKJV).

Persecution is not the problem. Sin is the problem. As believers, we're here to help people overcome it, even if it means risking our own lives. (From *Max on Life* by Max Lucado.)

REACTION

7. Why is it difficult to trust in God's goodness when you see suffering in the world?

_____

_____

_____

8. Why is it difficult to trust in God's goodness when you are facing persecution?

_____

_____

_____

9. Why are persecution and suffering inevitable in the life of a believer?

_____

_____

_____

10. Why do you think God allows his followers to endure hardships?

_____

_____

_____

11. How can the example of Jesus and Paul help you to persevere during trials?

_____

_____

_____

12. How can you encourage others going through difficulties and help them see that God is always good?

_____

_____

_____

LIFE LESSONS

We come into this world trusting in the goodness of others. Even though we aren't aware of our dependency at the time, we would not have survived without them. Some of us were fortunate to have loving parents. Others had adoptive parents or guardians who took care of us. As we grew, we learned that when we experienced troubles and our hearts were grieved, we could trust in a doctor, or a counselor, or a pastor, or a good friend for help. Like Asaph, we also came to understand that we could trust in the goodness of God. In spite of the sufferings we witnessed, or the wickedness of others, as we drew near to God we found that he drew near to us. Like Asaph, we never have to fear that we will be abandoned. God is always with us.

DEVOTION

Father, our hearts are often grieved by the suffering and evil we see in this world. Help us to always rely on your goodness and trust that you have a plan for our lives. Help us to experience your presence each day. Give us more courage as we look to you—the one who knows no fear.

JOURNALING

What problem do you need to turn over to God and trust that he will handle it for you?

_____

_____

_____

_____

_____

_____

_____

_____

_____

_____

FOR FURTHER READING

To complete the book of Psalms during this twelve-part study, read Psalms 65–76. For more Bible passages about the goodness of God, read Exodus 33:18–19; Micah 6:6–8; Mark 10:17–18; Romans 8:26–28; Galatians 5:22–25; 1 Timothy 4:4–5; James 1:16–18; and 1 John 1:5.

EMBRACING GOD'S LAW

*If they break My statutes and do not keep
My commandments, then I will punish their
transgression. . . . Nevertheless My lovingkindness
I will not utterly take from him.*
PSALM 89:31–33 NKJV

REFLECTION

Think of a particular time when you were challenged or comforted by a verse or passage in the Bible. How do you sense God speaking to you? How did that affect your life?

_____

_____

_____

_____

SITUATION

Ethan the Ezrahite, the author of Psalm 89, was evidently a counselor in King Solomon's court. He was known for his great wisdom, for the Bible holds him up as a standard of comparison to Solomon: "He was wiser than anyone else, including Ethan the Ezrahite" (1 Kings 4:31). Some believe he might have been the same person as Jeduthun or one of his descendants. In this psalm, Ethan reflects on the covenant that God established with King David and the great love the Lord has shown to his people. But also laments over the fact that David's descendants often forsook God's law and did not follow his commands. In spite of this, Ethan states his assurance that God has not removed his love from Israel, nor will he ever break the promises made to his people.

OBSERVATION

Read Psalm 89:19–37 from the New International
Version or the New King James Version.

NEW INTERNATIONAL VERSION
¹⁹ Once you spoke in a vision,
  to your faithful people you said:

"I have bestowed strength on a warrior;
    I have raised up a young man from among the people.
²⁰ I have found David my servant;
    with my sacred oil I have anointed him.
²¹ My hand will sustain him;
    surely my arm will strengthen him.
²² The enemy will not get the better of him;
    the wicked will not oppress him.
²³ I will crush his foes before him
    and strike down his adversaries.
²⁴ My faithful love will be with him,
    and through my name his horn will be exalted.
²⁵ I will set his hand over the sea,
    his right hand over the rivers.
²⁶ He will call out to me, 'You are my Father,
    my God, the Rock my Savior.'
²⁷ And I will appoint him to be my firstborn,
    the most exalted of the kings of the earth.
²⁸ I will maintain my love to him forever,
    and my covenant with him will never fail.
²⁹ I will establish his line forever,
    his throne as long as the heavens endure.

³⁰ "If his sons forsake my law
    and do not follow my statutes,
³¹ if they violate my decrees
    and fail to keep my commands,
³² I will punish their sin with the rod,
    their iniquity with flogging;
³³ but I will not take my love from him,
    nor will I ever betray my faithfulness.
³⁴ I will not violate my covenant
    or alter what my lips have uttered.

³⁵ Once for all, I have sworn by my holiness—
   and I will not lie to David—
³⁶ that his line will continue forever
   and his throne endure before me like the sun;
³⁷ it will be established forever like the moon,
   the faithful witness in the sky."

New King James Version
¹⁹ Then You spoke in a vision to Your holy one,
And said: "I have given help to one who is mighty;
I have exalted one chosen from the people.
²⁰ I have found My servant David;
With My holy oil I have anointed him,
²¹ With whom My hand shall be established;
Also My arm shall strengthen him.
²² The enemy shall not outwit him,
Nor the son of wickedness afflict him.
²³ I will beat down his foes before his face,
And plague those who hate him.

²⁴ "But My faithfulness and My mercy shall be with him,
And in My name his horn shall be exalted.
²⁵ Also I will set his hand over the sea,
And his right hand over the rivers.
²⁶ He shall cry to Me, 'You are my Father,
My God, and the rock of my salvation.'
²⁷ Also I will make him My firstborn,
The highest of the kings of the earth.
²⁸ My mercy I will keep for him forever,
And My covenant shall stand firm with him.
²⁹ His seed also I will make to endure forever,
And his throne as the days of heaven.

[30] "If his sons forsake My law

And do not walk in My judgments,

[31] If they break My statutes

And do not keep My commandments,

[32] Then I will punish their transgression with the rod,

And their iniquity with stripes.

[33] Nevertheless My lovingkindness I will not utterly take from him,

Nor allow My faithfulness to fail.

[34] My covenant I will not break,

Nor alter the word that has gone out of My lips.

[35] Once I have sworn by My holiness;

I will not lie to David:

[36] His seed shall endure forever,

And his throne as the sun before Me;

[37] It shall be established forever like the moon,

Even like the faithful witness in the sky." *Selah*

EXPLORATION

1. What promises had God made to his servant David?

_____

_____

_____

_____

2. What does the psalmist state will happen to those who do not follow God's laws?

_____

_____

_____

3. What rewards are given to those who remain faithful to God's laws?

_____

_____

_____

4. What attitude should you have toward God's laws in the Bible?

_____

_____

_____

5. How did the psalmist know that God would never "take his love" away from his people?

_____

_____

_____

6. Why is it important to follow God's commands regardless of what others are doing?

_____

_____

_____

INSPIRATION

The Ten Commandments tell us not to covet or lust. However, all moral law is more than a test; it's for our own good. Every law which God has given has been for our benefit. If a person breaks it, he is not only rebelling against God, he is hurting himself. God gave "the law" because he loves man. It is for man's benefit. God's commandments were given to protect and promote man's happiness, not to restrict it. God wants the best for man. To ask God to revise his commandments would be to ask him to stop loving man.

Children usually accuse their parents of "not understanding" and being too strict. When a father says to his teenager, "Be in at eleven o'clock, and let me know exactly where you are going to be," he is protecting his child, not punishing him. God is a loving father.

When Adam and Eve broke God's commandment, they died spiritually and faced eternal death. The consequences of that act were immediate and fearful. Sin became, and is, the stubborn fact of life.

In our universe, we live under God's law. In the physical realm, the planets move in split-second precision. There is no guesswork in the galaxies. We see in nature that everything is part of a plan which is harmonious, orderly, and obedient. Could a God who made the physical universe be any less exacting in the higher spiritual and moral order? God loves us with an infinite love, but he cannot and will not approve of disorder. Consequently, he has laid down spiritual laws which, if obeyed, bring harmony and fulfillment, but, if disobeyed, bring discord and disorder. (From *How to Be Born Again* by Billy Graham.)

REACTION

7. What are some of the "laws" that you live under every day?

8. How do the laws that God established in the Bible reveal the great love he has for you?

9. How do God's laws show that he cannot—and will not—approve of disorder?

_____

_____

_____

10. What blessings have you enjoyed as a result of obeying God's Word?

_____

_____

_____

11. In what situations are you tempted to break God's law?

_____

_____

_____

12. How can you gain strength from God's Word to overcome temptation?

_____

_____

_____

LIFE LESSONS

Words build relationships. Think of a young couple talking endlessly about everything. Using mere puffs of wind that send sound waves through the air, they are intermingling their hearts and minds, causing their thoughts to become words. The Bible declares that God also speaks. The book of Genesis opens with a repetitive, "God said . . ." (1:3, 6, 9, 11, 14, 20, 24, 26, 29). God, our Creator, desires to be in living relationship with us—and our living God speaks through his Word. Furthermore, the Bible introduces us to the _Living Word_ . . . who is Jesus, the Son of God. Sins breaks our relationship with God, but Jesus, through his redeeming work on the cross, restores that relationship. The Bible is all about growing in an abundant relationship with God. The way that we build that relationship is to stay faithful and true to his commands.

DEVOTION

Father, we're amazed at your love for us. You have shown us the way to find true happiness and fulfillment. You have shown us how precious your Word is in our lives. Enrich our conscience today so that we may remain faithful to always obey you.

JOURNALING

In what areas of your life do you need to better embrace God's law? How will you do this?

_____

_____

_____

_____

_____

_____

_____

_____

_____

_____

_____

_____

_____

_____

FOR FURTHER READING

To complete the book of Psalms during this twelve-part study, read Psalms 77–89. For more Bible passages about embracing God's law, read Exodus 15:26–27; 20:1–17; Leviticus 20:22–24; Joshua 1:7–9; Romans 7:7–12; Galatians 2:15–16; James 2:8–11; and 1 John 3:4–6.

THE RIGHT PERSPECTIVE

*Teach us to number our days, that we
may gain a heart of wisdom.*
PSALM 90:12

REFLECTION

How do you cheer yourself up when you feel discontent or dissatisfied with life?

_____

_____

_____

_____

SITUATION

Moses, the author of Psalm 90, was the great lawgiver and leader of the Hebrew people during the exodus from Egypt. While this is the only psalm credited to him, Jewish tradition holds that he was also the author of the books of the Torah (Genesis–Deuteronomy). The spirit of Moses' concern is certainly prevalent in the psalm, which focuses on the transient nature of life in this world, making the most of our days by living in a way that is pleasing to God (and free of his judgment), and seeking God's favor as we do the work he has prepared for us. Moses' words remind us that we need to "number our days" (Psalm 90:12) and have the right perspective on life. As Solomon concluded, "Now all has been heard; here is the conclusion of the matter: Fear God and keep his commandments, for this is the duty of all mankind" (Ecclesiastes 12:13).

OBSERVATION

Read Psalm 90:1–12 from the New International
Version or the New King James Version.

New International Version
[1] Lord, you have been our dwelling place
    throughout all generations.
[2] Before the mountains were born

or you brought forth the whole world,
from everlasting to everlasting you are God.

3 You turn people back to dust,
saying, "Return to dust, you mortals."
4 A thousand years in your sight
are like a day that has just gone by,
or like a watch in the night.
5 Yet you sweep people away in the sleep of death—
they are like the new grass of the morning:
6 In the morning it springs up new,
but by evening it is dry and withered.

7 We are consumed by your anger
and terrified by your indignation.
8 You have set our iniquities before you,
our secret sins in the light of your presence.
9 All our days pass away under your wrath;
we finish our years with a moan.
10 Our days may come to seventy years,
or eighty, if our strength endures;
yet the best of them are but trouble and sorrow,
for they quickly pass, and we fly away.
11 If only we knew the power of your anger!
Your wrath is as great as the fear that is your due.
12 Teach us to number our days,
that we may gain a heart of wisdom.

New King James Version
1 Lord, You have been our dwelling place in all generations.
2 Before the mountains were brought forth,
Or ever You had formed the earth and the world,
Even from everlasting to everlasting, You are God.

³ You turn man to destruction,
And say, "Return, O children of men."
⁴ For a thousand years in Your sight
Are like yesterday when it is past,
And like a watch in the night.
⁵ You carry them away like a flood;
They are like a sleep.
In the morning they are like grass which grows up:
⁶ In the morning it flourishes and grows up;
In the evening it is cut down and withers.

⁷ For we have been consumed by Your anger,
And by Your wrath we are terrified.
⁸ You have set our iniquities before You,
Our secret sins in the light of Your countenance.
⁹ For all our days have passed away in Your wrath;
We finish our years like a sigh.
¹⁰ The days of our lives are seventy years;
And if by reason of strength they are eighty years,
Yet their boast is only labor and sorrow;
For it is soon cut off, and we fly away.
¹¹ Who knows the power of Your anger?
For as the fear of You, so is Your wrath.
¹² So teach us to number our days,
That we may gain a heart of wisdom.

EXPLORATION

1. What did Moses want his readers to understand about God? About themselves? About life?

_____

_____

_____

2. How does Moses contrast God with people in this passage?

_____

_____

_____

3. Why does God address the sin of his people?

_____

_____

4. What does it mean to fear God?

_____

_____

_____

5. Why is it important to remember that life is short?

_____

_____

_____

6. How do Moses' words help you to have the right perspective about life?

_____

_____

_____

INSPIRATION

Contrast two workers. The first one slices the air with his hand, making points, instructing the crowd. He is a teacher and, from the look of things, a compelling one. He stands on a beach, rendering the slanted seashore an amphitheater. As he talks, his audience increases; as the audience grows, his platform shrinks. The instructor steps back and back until the next step will take him into the water. That's when he spots another worker.

A fisherman. Not animated, but frustrated. He spent all night fishing, but caught nothing. All night! Double-digit hours' worth of casting, splashing, and pulling the net. But he caught nothing. Unlike the teacher, the fisherman has nothing to show for his work. He draws no crowds; he doesn't even draw fish. Just nets.

Two workers. One pumped up. One worn out. The first, fruitful. The second, futile. To which do you relate?...

God's eyes fall on the work of our hands. Our Wednesdays matter to him as much as our Sundays. He blurs the secular and sacred.... With God, our work matters as much as our worship. Indeed, work can be worship.

Peter wrote: "You are a chosen people, a royal priesthood, a holy nation, God's special possession, that you may declare the praises of him who called you out of darkness into his wonderful light" (1 Peter 2:9).

Next time a job application requests your prior employment, write "priest" or "priestess," for you are one. A priest represents God, and you, my friend, represent God. So "let every detail in your lives—words, actions, whatever—be done in the name of the Master, Jesus" (Colossians 3:17 MSG). (From *Cure for the Common Life* by Max Lucado.)

REACTION

7. Why do some people feel discontent and disillusioned with life?

_____

_____

_____

_____

8. How do Moses' words in Psalm 90 encourage you to cope with the monotony of life?

_____

_____

_____

9. What steps can you take that will refresh you when you grow discouraged?

_____

_____

_____

10. How has staying focused on God and his plan for your life helped you stay motivated?

_____

_____

_____

11. What are some ways you have seen God "balancing" out the good with the bad?

_____

_____

_____

12. What causes you to worry about your future? How will you take those worries to God?

_____

_____

_____

LIFE LESSONS

A seminary professor, using the metrics that insurance companies use, once calculated as best he could the day that he would die. Morbid? Perhaps . . . but wise. The professor did not want to waste a single day. In the same way, Moses asked God, "Teach us to number our days, that we may gain a heart of wisdom" (Psalm 90:12). The Bible repeatedly reminds us that life is short. As James writes, "You are a mist that appears for a little while and then vanishes" (4:14). The time we are "killing" is gone forever. For this reason, it is important for us to use our days wisely. As Moses writes, we do this by seeking a heart of wisdom—by asking God to fill us with "the Spirit of wisdom and of understanding" that Jesus himself possessed (Isaiah 11:2). As we gain this wisdom from God, we learn to focus our priorities on what matters for eternity.

DEVOTION

Father, the monotony of life can lull us into a sense of dissatisfaction and futility. In those times, remind us that you are in control and you have a purpose for us. Give us your perspective of what is important and help us to invest our time wisely. Take our efforts for your kingdom and transform them into works that will last for eternity.

JOURNALING

What are some of the pursuits you have that are building God's kingdom?

_____

_____

_____

_____

_____

_____

_____

FOR FURTHER READING

To complete the book of Psalms during this twelve-part study, read Psalms 90–101. For more Bible passages about having the right perspective, read Matthew 6:19–21; John 4:35–38; 15:16; Colossians 1:10–12; 1 Timothy 4:16; 6:17–19; 2 Thessalonians 1:11; and Hebrews 10:34–36.

GETTING OUR PRIORITIES STRAIGHT

Bless the LORD, O my soul, and forget not all His benefits:
Who forgives all your iniquities, who heals all your diseases . . .
who crowns you with lovingkindness and tender mercies.
PSALM 103:2–4 NKJV

REFLECTION

What are some of your greatest priorities right now? How are you pursuing those priorities?

_____

_____

_____

_____

_____

_____

_____

_____

SITUATION

King David, the author of Psalm 103, was a man who had many responsibilities and many priorities in life. When those priorities included God, he was successful in what he did, from slaying the giant Goliath, to eluding capture by King Saul, to assuming the throne of Israel and vanquishing the nation's enemies. But when David became complacent in his role—when he allowed the familiarity of day-to-day palace life to distract him—negative consequences soon followed. In one notable instance, "In the spring, at the time when kings go off to war . . . David remained in Jerusalem" (2 Samuel 11:1). What followed, of course, was David's adulterous affair with Bathsheba . . . and soon after, his beloved son Absalom staged a revolt against him. Yet even in these times of distress, David knew that if he refocused his priorities on God, the Lord would be compassionate and forgive him. "As a father has compassion on his children," he wrote, "so the LORD has compassion on those who fear him" (Psalm 103:13).

OBSERVATION

Read Psalm 103:1–14 from the New International
Version or the New King James Version.

NEW INTERNATIONAL VERSION

¹ Praise the LORD, my soul;
  all my inmost being, praise his holy name.
² Praise the LORD, my soul,
  and forget not all his benefits—
³ who forgives all your sins
  and heals all your diseases,
⁴ who redeems your life from the pit
  and crowns you with love and compassion,
⁵ who satisfies your desires with good things
  so that your youth is renewed like the eagle's.

⁶ The LORD works righteousness
  and justice for all the oppressed.

⁷ He made known his ways to Moses,
  his deeds to the people of Israel:
⁸ The LORD is compassionate and gracious,
  slow to anger, abounding in love.
⁹ He will not always accuse,
  nor will he harbor his anger forever;
¹⁰ he does not treat us as our sins deserve
  or repay us according to our iniquities.
¹¹ For as high as the heavens are above the earth,
  so great is his love for those who fear him;
¹² as far as the east is from the west,
  so far has he removed our transgressions from us.

¹³ As a father has compassion on his children,

so the LORD has compassion on those who fear him;

¹⁴ for he knows how we are formed,

he remembers that we are dust.

NEW KING JAMES VERSION

¹ Bless the LORD, O my soul;

And all that is within me, bless His holy name!

² Bless the LORD, O my soul,

And forget not all His benefits:

³ Who forgives all your iniquities,

Who heals all your diseases,

⁴ Who redeems your life from destruction,

Who crowns you with lovingkindness and tender mercies,

⁵ Who satisfies your mouth with good things,

So that your youth is renewed like the eagle's.

⁶ The LORD executes righteousness

And justice for all who are oppressed.

⁷ He made known His ways to Moses,

His acts to the children of Israel.

⁸ The LORD is merciful and gracious,

Slow to anger, and abounding in mercy.

⁹ He will not always strive with us,

Nor will He keep His anger forever.

¹⁰ He has not dealt with us according to our sins,

Nor punished us according to our iniquities.

¹¹ For as the heavens are high above the earth,

So great is His mercy toward those who fear Him;

¹² As far as the east is from the west,

So far has He removed our transgressions from us.

¹³ As a father pities his children,

So the LORD pities those who fear Him.
[14] For He knows our frame;
He remembers that we are dust.

EXPLORATION

1. Why is it critical, in the daily stresses of life, to "forget not" all of God's blessings?

_____

_____

_____

_____

2. What are some ways that David expresses his praise to God for his blessings?

_____

_____

_____

_____

3. What do you learn about God's character from this psalm?

_____

_____

_____

_____

4. What does David say about the way God treats our transgressions when we confess our sins and repent of them?

_____

_____

_____

5. Why is it comforting to know that God "remembers that we are dust" (verse 14)?

_____

_____

_____

_____

_____

6. What are some of the ways that God helps you to refocus your priorities on him?

_____

_____

_____

_____

_____

INSPIRATION

Abraham Lincoln once listened to the pleas of the mother of a soldier who'd been sentenced to hang for treason. She begged the President to grant a pardon. Lincoln agreed. Yet, he's reported to have left the lady with the following words: "Still, I wish we could teach him a lesson. I wish we could give him just a little bit of a hangin'."

I think I know what the old rail-splitter had in mind. . . . Our family was having Sunday lunch at the home of a fellow missionary family. It was after the meal, and I was in the kitchen while Denalyn and our friends Paul and Debbie were talking in the living room. Their three-year-old daughter Beth Ann was playing with our two-year-old Jenna in the front yard. All of a sudden, Beth Ann rushed in with a look of panic on her face. "Jenna is in the pool!"

Paul was the first to arrive at the poolside . . . and lifted her up out of the water to the extended hands of her mother. Jenna was simultaneously choking, crying, and coughing. She vomited a bellyful of water. I held her as she cried. Denalyn began to weep. I began to sweat.

For the rest of the day I couldn't hold her enough, nor could we thank Beth Ann enough (we took her out for ice cream). I still can't thank God enough. It was a little bit of hangin'.

The stool was kicked out from under my feet and the rope jerked around my neck just long enough to remind me of what really matters. It was a divine slap, a gracious knock on the head, a severe mercy. Because of it, I came face to face with one of the underground's slyest agents—the agent of familiarity. . . .

To say that this agent of familiarity breeds contempt is to let him off easy. Contempt is just one of his offspring. He also sires broken hearts, wasted hours, and an insatiable desire for more. . . . He won't take your children, he'll just make you too busy to notice them. His whispers to procrastinate are seductive. There is always next summer to coach the team, next month to go to the lake, and next week to teach Johnny how to pray.

He'll make you forget that the faces around your table will soon be at tables of their own. Hence, books will go unread, games will go unplayed, hearts will go unnurtured, and opportunities will go ignored. All because the poison of the ordinary has deadened your senses to the magic of the moment. . . .

On a shelf above my desk is a picture of two little girls. They're holding hands and standing in front of a swimming pool, the same pool from which the younger of the two had been pulled only minutes before. I put the picture where I would see it daily so I would remember what God doesn't want me to forget.

And you can bet this time I'm going to remember. I don't want any more hangin'. Not even a little bit. (From *God Came Near* by Max Lucado.)

REACTION

7. How can familiarity divert your focus from life's most important things?

_____

_____

_____

_____

8. What happens when you give in to "the agent of familiarity" and neglect the important things in life?

_____

_____

_____

9. David's words in Psalm 103 recount many of the blessings that God had given to his people. Why is it important to reflect on these types of past blessings from God?

_____

_____

_____

10. Why do you think it is easy to overlook thanking God for all he has done?

_____

_____

_____

11. How can you remember to praise God this week for what he has done for you?

_____

_____

_____

_____

12. How will you express your praise to God for all the compassion he has extended to you?

_____

_____

_____

_____

LIFE LESSONS

It's easy to overlook the familiar in life. The Styrofoam cup that is mindlessly tossed in the trash. The crystal glass, a wedding gift, that sits in the lighted hutch near the dining room. But what if that Styrofoam cup were used to get critically needed medication into a dying person? What if the crystal glass served as a reminder to a man who had lost his wife of their happy marriage? Suddenly, the overlooked becomes important. David reminds us in this psalm to "forget not all [God's] benefits" or take anything for granted (Psalm 103:2). God invests everything with value—even turning ashes into beauty (see Isaiah 61:3). As Paul writes, "In all things God works for the good" (Romans 8:28), even the mundane. So never overlook the simple everyday blessings of God—forgiveness, mercy, rest, comfort—and praise the Lord for them.

DEVOTION

Lord, it is easy to become complacent in our faith and forget all of the everyday mercies that you extend to us. Please help us to focus our priorities on you and to not forget all of your blessings. You are worthy of our praise, and we thank you and worship your holy name.

JOURNALING

What changes do you need to make this week in your priorities?

_____

_____

_____

_____

_____

_____

_____

_____

_____

_____

_____

_____

_____

FOR FURTHER READING

To complete the book of Psalms during this twelve-part study, read Psalms 102–114. For more Bible passages about remembering God's blessings and putting him first, read Deuteronomy 6:10–13; 1 Chronicles 16:9–12; Job 36:24; Psalm 33:1; 77:11; 147:1; Matthew 6:33–34; Luke 10:38–42; and 1 Timothy 6:17–19.

GOD'S PROTECTION AND SALVATION

Those who trust in the LORD are like Mount Zion, which cannot be shaken but endures forever. As the mountains surround Jerusalem, so the LORD surrounds his people.

PSALM 125:1–2

REFLECTION

What are some routines you have developed that help you remember God's promises?

_____

_____

_____

_____

SITUATION

Psalms 125 and 126, by an unknown writer, are part of a collection known as the "Song of Ascents." Most likely, these songs were sung by the Jewish pilgrims as they "ascended" from the countryside to Jerusalem to attend the three required annual festivals. As God had commanded his people in the days of Moses, "Three times a year all your men must appear before the LORD your God at the place he will choose: at the Festival of Unleavened Bread, the Festival of Weeks and the Festival of Tabernacles" (Deuteronomy 16:16). Psalms 125 and 126 would have reminded the pilgrims of their history as they traveled into Jerusalem and how the Lord had faithfully guided them. As psalms of "communal confidence," they expressed the pilgrims' trust in the Lord to continually meet their needs and protect them.

OBSERVATION

Read Psalms 125:1–126:6 from the New International
Version or the New King James Version.

NEW INTERNATIONAL VERSION
125:1 Those who trust in the LORD are like Mount Zion,
　　which cannot be shaken but endures forever.

² As the mountains surround Jerusalem,
  so the LORD surrounds his people
  both now and forevermore.

³ The scepter of the wicked will not remain
  over the land allotted to the righteous,
for then the righteous might use
  their hands to do evil.

⁴ LORD, do good to those who are good,
  to those who are upright in heart.
⁵ But those who turn to crooked ways
  the LORD will banish with the evildoers.

Peace be on Israel.

¹²⁶:¹ When the LORD restored the fortunes of Zion,
  we were like those who dreamed.
² Our mouths were filled with laughter,
  our tongues with songs of joy.
Then it was said among the nations,
  "The LORD has done great things for them."
³ The LORD has done great things for us,
  and we are filled with joy.

⁴ Restore our fortunes, LORD,
  like streams in the Negev.
⁵ Those who sow with tears
  will reap with songs of joy.
⁶ Those who go out weeping,
  carrying seed to sow,
will return with songs of joy,
  carrying sheaves with them.

NEW KING JAMES VERSION

^{125:1} Those who trust in the LORD
Are like Mount Zion,
Which cannot be moved, but abides forever.
² As the mountains surround Jerusalem,
So the LORD surrounds His people
From this time forth and forever.
³ For the scepter of wickedness shall not rest
On the land allotted to the righteous,
Lest the righteous reach out their hands to iniquity.

⁴ Do good, O LORD, to those who are good,
And to those who are upright in their hearts.

⁵ As for such as turn aside to their crooked ways,
The LORD shall lead them away
With the workers of iniquity.

Peace be upon Israel!

^{126:1} When the LORD brought back the captivity of Zion,
We were like those who dream.
² Then our mouth was filled with laughter,
And our tongue with singing.
Then they said among the nations,
"The LORD has done great things for them."
³ The LORD has done great things for us,
And we are glad.

⁴ Bring back our captivity, O LORD,
As the streams in the South.

⁵ Those who sow in tears

Shall reap in joy.
[6] He who continually goes forth weeping,
Bearing seed for sowing,
Shall doubtless come again with rejoicing,
Bringing his sheaves with him.

EXPLORATION

1. How does the psalmist describe the protection of God in these verses?

_____

_____

_____

_____

_____

_____

_____

2. What does the psalmist ask God to do to the righteous? To the wicked?

_____

_____

_____

_____

_____

_____

_____

3. Why can you be confident that good will ultimately defeat evil?

_____

_____

_____

_____

_____

4. How does God want you to respond to his offer of salvation and protection?

_____

_____

_____

_____

_____

5. What happens when people publicly acknowledge what God has done for them?

_____

_____

_____

_____

_____

6. How have you seen God turn cries of weeping into "songs of joy" (Psalm 126:6)?

_____

_____

_____

_____

_____

INSPIRATION

At the moment of Jesus' death, an unbelievable miracle occurred. "Jesus cried out with a loud voice, and breathed His last. Then the veil of the temple was torn in two from top to bottom" (Mark 15:37–38 NKJV).

According to Henry and Richard Blackaby, "The veil separated the people from the temple's Most Holy Place, and it had done so for centuries. According to tradition, the veil—a handbreadth in thickness—was woven of seventy-two twisted plaits, each plait consisting of twenty-four threads. The veil was apparently sixty feet long and thirty feet wide."

We aren't talking about small, delicate drapes. This curtain was a wall made of fabric. The fact that it was torn from top to bottom reveals that the hands behind the deed were divine. God himself grasped the curtain and ripped it in two. No more!

No more division. No more separation. No more sacrifices. "No condemnation for those who are in Christ Jesus" (Romans 8:1). "'[Jesus] himself bore our sins' in his body on the cross, so that we might die to sins and live for righteousness; 'by his wounds you have been healed'" (1 Peter 2:24).

Heaven's work of redemption was finished. Christ's death brought new life. Whatever barrier that had separated—or might ever separate—us from God was gone.

Gone is the fear of falling short! Gone is the anxious quest for right behavior. Gone are the nagging questions: *Have I done enough? Am I good enough? Will I achieve enough?* The legalist finds rest. The atheist finds hope. The God of Abraham is not a God of burdens but a God of rest. (From *Unshakable Hope* by Max Lucado.)

REACTION

7. What is significant about God tearing the curtain in the temple from top to bottom at the moment of Jesus' death?

_____

_____

_____

_____

_____

8. What are some ways that people try to earn their way into heaven?

9. Why is it difficult to accept salvation as a free gift?

10. Why is not making a choice to accept God's gift actually a choice to reject his offer?

11. What prompted you to seek God's forgiveness and salvation?

12. Which of your friends or co-workers does not fully understand God's plan of salvation? How can you share the gospel with that person?

_____

_____

_____

_____

_____

_____

LIFE LESSONS

Today, protection is serious business. People in nations around the world spend billions of dollars on home protection. TSA checkpoints populate our airports. Companies have sprung up to offer online security protection from identity theft. We all want to be safe. The people of Israel wanted the same . . . and they knew they had the Lord God as their protector. "As the mountains surround Jerusalem," the psalmist wrote, "so the LORD surrounds his people both now and forevermore" (Psalm 125:2). Of course, this doesn't mean that only good things happened to them. History tells us the Jewish people endured one trial after another. But they knew nothing could take them out of the Lord's hands. The same is true of us. Trials, suffering, and even death will come our way. Yet, we can know that because of Jesus' saving work on the cross, we are protected from eternal judgment. Glory and eternal life are in our future.

DEVOTION

Father, our hearts are filled with joy because of the great things you have done for us. We thank you for your salvation, for your constant provision, and your continual protection. We offer you today our praise, our adoration, and our thanksgiving.

JOURNALING

What are some ways that you have seen God protect your life?

_____

_____

_____

_____

_____

_____

_____

_____

_____

_____

_____

_____

_____

_____

_____

_____

_____

_____

_____

_____

FOR FURTHER READING

To complete the book of Psalms during this twelve-part study, read Psalms 115–126. For more Bible passages about God's salvation, read 1 Chronicles 16:23–24; Psalms 40:10–16; 69:29–33; Isaiah 12:2–3; Jonah 2:7–9; Acts 4:11–12; 1 Thessalonians 5:4–10; and Revelation 7:9–12.

GOD'S BLESSINGS ON FAMILIES

Like arrows in the hand of a warrior, so are the children of one's youth. Happy is the man who has his quiver full of them.

PSALM 127:4–5 NKJV

REFLECTION

Think of one of your favorite childhood memories. Why is that memory special to you?

_____

_____

_____

_____

SITUATION

Solomon, the author of Psalm 127, was the son of King David and ruled Israel during the time of its greatest prosperity and independence (c. 970–931 BC). Although only two psalms are credited to him, Jewish tradition holds that he also contributed to the Book of Proverbs and wrote Song of Songs and Ecclesiastes. The Bible credits Solomon as being one of the wisest men who ever lived and for building the first Temple in Jerusalem. In Psalm 127, one of the "Songs of Ascents," Solomon perhaps reflects on these building efforts, noting that unless God is in the process of all our human efforts, "the builders labor in vain" (verse 1). Solomon also notes that "children are a heritage from the LORD," (verse 3), and even today this psalm is often recited in Jewish culture as part of a thanksgiving service following the birth of a child.

OBSERVATION

Read Psalm 127:1–5 from the New International Version or the New King James Version.

NEW INTERNATIONAL VERSION
[1] Unless the LORD builds the house,
   the builders labor in vain.

Unless the LORD watches over the city,
    the guards stand watch in vain.
2 In vain you rise early
    and stay up late,
toiling for food to eat—
    for he grants sleep to those he loves.

3 Children are a heritage from the LORD,
    offspring a reward from him.
4 Like arrows in the hands of a warrior
    are children born in one's youth.
5 Blessed is the man
    whose quiver is full of them.
They will not be put to shame
    when they contend with their opponents in court.

NEW KING JAMES VERSION
1 Unless the LORD builds the house,
They labor in vain who build it;
Unless the LORD guards the city,
The watchman stays awake in vain.
2 It is vain for you to rise up early,
To sit up late,
To eat the bread of sorrows;
For so He gives His beloved sleep.

3 Behold, children are a heritage from the LORD,
The fruit of the womb is a reward.
4 Like arrows in the hand of a warrior,
So are the children of one's youth.
5 Happy is the man who has his quiver full of them;
They shall not be ashamed,
But shall speak with their enemies in the gate.

EXPLORATION

1. What does Solomon say about our human efforts?

_____

_____

_____

_____

2. What does Solomon say about our efforts to protect our homes and families?

_____

_____

_____

3. What is the only true way to live an anxiety-free existence?

_____

_____

_____

4. How does Solomon say that we are to view our children?

_____

_____

_____

5. What good things does God want families to enjoy?

_____

_____

_____

6. How can families determine whether God is the head of their home?

_____

_____

INSPIRATION

The psalmist says we are "blessed" if our "quiver is full of children" (see Psalm 127:4–5). . . . The "arrows" God delivers into our quiver come ready-made, needed to be shaped and pointed toward the right target. . . .

The most taxing of all are the years a family finds itself in and out of crisis situations. Little babies that cooed and gurgled grow up into challenging, independent-thinking adolescents. The protective, sheltered environment of the home is broken into by the school, new friends, alien philosophies, financial strain, illness, accidents, hard questions, constant decisions, and busy schedules. . . and it isn't difficult to feel the pressure mounting—especially when you add dating, new drivers in the family, leaving for college, talk of marriage, and moving out. Whew! And what does God say about these years? . . .

He says we'll be "blessed." We'll be "happy." It will "be well" with us during these years. A dream? No. Remember this is a domestic mural, one scene growing out of the former and leading into the next. In the family portrayed on this scriptural canvas, the Lord is still central. When children come, they are viewed as a gift of the Lord, a reward, fruit provided by him. . . .

It may be the right time for you to come to terms with the truth regarding your family. I must be honest with you, in most of the family conflicts I have dealt with involving trouble with teenagers, the problem has been more with parents who were either too liberal and permissive or too inflexible, distant, rigid (and sometimes hypocritical) than with teenagers who were unwilling to cooperate. When the modeling is as it should be, there is seldom much trouble from those who fall under the shadow of the leader.

Strengthening your grip on the family may start with an unguarded appraisal of the leadership your family is expected to follow. (From *Strengthening Your Grip* by Charles Swindoll.)

REACTION

7. What are some of the ways the "arrows" (children) whom God delivers into a family need to be "shaped and pointed toward the right target"?

_____

_____

_____

_____

8. How can families work to strengthen family relationships?

_____

_____

_____

9. What encouragement can families glean from Solomon's words in this psalm?

_____

_____

_____

10. What happens to families who don't follow God's ways?

_____

_____

_____

11. How can parents teach their children to respect God?

_____

_____

_____

12. How has God blessed your family? How do you praise him for his blessings?

_____

_____

_____

_____

_____

_____

LIFE LESSONS

Parental joy is like no other in the world . . . and parental pain knows no rival. Cradling a newborn in our arms provokes glistening tears of delight. The teenage years produce tears of frustration. At times we may wonder if the psalmist was in his right mind when he said we are "blessed" for having them. But as we look at passages of Scripture such as Psalm 127, we find that God truly loves families, blesses families, celebrates families. Jesus entered this world as one of us and was born into a family. The Trinity is the proto-Family with Father, Son, and Holy Spirit. And God is creating his own family, as Paul reveals: "For this reason I kneel before the Father, from whom every family in heaven and on earth derives its name" (Ephesians 3:14–15). The name God desires to be called the most is "Father." As Jesus taught, "This, then, is how you should pray: 'Our Father in heaven, hallowed be your name'" (Matthew 6:9).

DEVOTION

God, give us strength as we try to be more like Jesus in our homes. We ask you to keep the evil one away from us and draw us into close communion with you. Let our families be testimonies of your love for us so that when people look at us, they will see how you have loved the world.

JOURNALING

How can you ensure that God is the head of your home?

_____

_____

_____

_____

_____

_____

_____

_____

_____

_____

_____

_____

_____

_____

_____

_____

_____

_____

_____

FOR FURTHER READING

To complete the book of Psalms during this twelve-part study, read Psalms 127–138. For more Bible passages about families, read Genesis 2:18–24; Exodus 20:12; Deuteronomy 6:6–9; Psalm 101:1–3; Matthew 19:4–6; Acts 16:31–34; Ephesians 5:22–6:4; and 1 Timothy 3:4–5.

A LIFE OF PURPOSE

Your eyes saw my unformed body; all the days ordained for me were written in your book before one of them came to be.
PSALM 139:16

REFLECTION

When you reflect on your life, how have you seen that God had a plan and purpose for you?

_____

_____

_____

_____

SITUATION

The components of this psalm by David—consisting of a hymn, thanksgiving, and lament—reveal the depths of the personal relationship he had with the Lord. In many ways, the psalm captures David's realization as he looked back on his life and recognized that God was always there, always watching over him, and always aware of even his innermost thoughts, and always had a plan and purpose for his steps. While the idea of "God always watching" may make some people nervous, David praised God for his constant awareness, even offering, "Search me, God, and know my heart . . . see if there is any offensive way in me" (Psalm 139:23–24). David knew he was not perfect, but he also knew he was forgiven and restored. As he reflected on this, he couldn't help but worship his loving creator for the way he had guided him through life.

OBSERVATION

Read Psalm 139:7–24 from the New International
Version or the New King James Version.

New International Version
⁷ Where can I go from your Spirit?
   Where can I flee from your presence?

⁸ If I go up to the heavens, you are there;
if I make my bed in the depths, you are there.
⁹ If I rise on the wings of the dawn,
if I settle on the far side of the sea,
¹⁰ even there your hand will guide me,
your right hand will hold me fast.
¹¹ If I say, "Surely the darkness will hide me
and the light become night around me,"
¹² even the darkness will not be dark to you;
the night will shine like the day,
for darkness is as light to you.

¹³ For you created my inmost being;
you knit me together in my mother's womb.
¹⁴ I praise you because I am fearfully and wonderfully made;
your works are wonderful,
I know that full well.
¹⁵ My frame was not hidden from you
when I was made in the secret place,
when I was woven together in the depths of the earth.
¹⁶ Your eyes saw my unformed body;
all the days ordained for me were written in your book
before one of them came to be.
¹⁷ How precious to me are your thoughts, God!
How vast is the sum of them!
¹⁸ Were I to count them,
they would outnumber the grains of sand—
when I awake, I am still with you.
¹⁹ If only you, God, would slay the wicked!
Away from me, you who are bloodthirsty!
²⁰ They speak of you with evil intent;
your adversaries misuse your name.
²¹ Do I not hate those who hate you, LORD,

and abhor those who are in rebellion against you?
²² I have nothing but hatred for them;

I count them my enemies.
²³ Search me, God, and know my heart;

test me and know my anxious thoughts.
²⁴ See if there is any offensive way in me,

and lead me in the way everlasting.

New King James Version

⁷ Where can I go from Your Spirit?

Or where can I flee from Your presence?
⁸ If I ascend into heaven, You are there;

If I make my bed in hell, behold, You are there.
⁹ If I take the wings of the morning,

And dwell in the uttermost parts of the sea,
¹⁰ Even there Your hand shall lead me,

And Your right hand shall hold me.
¹¹ If I say, "Surely the darkness shall fall on me,"

Even the night shall be light about me;
¹² Indeed, the darkness shall not hide from You,

But the night shines as the day;

The darkness and the light are both alike to You.

¹³ For You formed my inward parts;

You covered me in my mother's womb.
¹⁴ I will praise You, for I am fearfully and wonderfully made;

Marvelous are Your works,

And that my soul knows very well.

¹⁵ My frame was not hidden from You,

When I was made in secret,

And skillfully wrought in the lowest parts of the earth.
¹⁶ Your eyes saw my substance, being yet unformed.

And in Your book they all were written,
The days fashioned for me,
When as yet there were none of them.
[17] How precious also are Your thoughts to me, O God!
How great is the sum of them!
[18] If I should count them, they would be more in number than the sand;
When I awake, I am still with You.

[19] Oh, that You would slay the wicked, O God!
Depart from me, therefore, you bloodthirsty men.
[20] For they speak against You wickedly;
Your enemies take Your name in vain.
[21] Do I not hate them, O LORD, who hate You?
And do I not loathe those who rise up against You?
[22] I hate them with perfect hatred;
I count them my enemies.

[23] Search me, O God, and know my heart;
Try me, and know my anxieties;
[24] And see if there is any wicked way in me,
And lead me in the way everlasting.

EXPLORATION

1. What does David say about the way in which God interacts with his children?

_____

_____

_____

_____

_____

2. How can you be sure that God knows what you are going through and cares about you?

_____

_____

_____

_____

_____

3. How can you be sure that God is with you always?

_____

_____

_____

_____

_____

4. Why is it impossible to hide your sins from God?

_____

_____

_____

_____

_____

5. What does David say about the plans that God has for your life?

_____

_____

_____

_____

_____

6. Why did David want God to "search" him and "test" him?

_____

_____

_____

_____

_____

INSPIRATION

You exited the womb uniquely equipped. David states it this way: "My frame was not hidden from You, when I was made in secret, and skillfully wrought in the lowest parts of the earth. Your eyes saw my substance, being yet unformed. And in Your book they all were written, the days fashioned for me, when as yet there were none of them" (Psalm 139:15–16 NKJV).

Spelunk these verses with me. David emphasizes the pronoun "you" as if to say "you, God, and you alone." "Made in secret" suggests a hidden and safe place, concealed from intruders and evil. Just as an artist takes a canvas into a locked studio, so God took you into His hidden chamber where you were "skillfully wrought."

Moses used the same word to describe the needlework of the tabernacle's inner curtains—stitched together by skillful hands for the highest purpose (see Exodus 26:1; 36:8; 38:9). The Master Weaver selected your temperament threads, your character texture, the yarn of your personality—all before you were born. God did not drop you into the world utterly defenseless and empty-handed. You arrived fully equipped.

"The days fashioned . . ." Day of birth and day of death. Days of difficulty and victory. What motivates you, what exhausts you . . . God authored—and authors—it all. . . .

My hands have never embroidered a stitch, but my mom's have. In pre-dishwasher days when mothers drafted young sons into kitchen duty to dry dishes, I grew too acquainted with her set of embroidered dishtowels. She had embellished sturdy white cloths with colorful threads: seven towels, each bearing the name of a different day. Her artisan skills rendered common towels uncommonly unique.

God did the same with you! . . . Don't dull your life by missing this point: You are more than statistical chance, more than a marriage of heredity and society, more than a confluence of inherited chromosomes and childhood trauma. More than a walking weather vane whipped about by the cold winds of fate. Thanks to God, you have been "sculpted from nothing into something" (verse 15 MSG). (From *Cure for the Common Life* by Max Lucado.)

REACTION

7. How can you be sure that you weren't an accident—that God knew you before you were born?

_____

_____

_____

_____

8. What are some of the ways that you have been "fully equipped" by God?

_____

_____

_____

_____

9. How does the fact that God has a plan for you impact the choices you make?

_____

_____

_____

_____

10. How comfortable are you in asking God to search you and know your heart? What reservations do you have about making this request?

_____

_____

_____

_____

11. How have you seen God purge your heart of "offensive ways"?

_____

_____

_____

12. What would you like God to reveal to you about his plans for your future?

_____

_____

LIFE LESSONS

David asked God to search his heart and reveal anything that was offensive to the Lord. In another psalm, he made this request: "Create in me a pure heart" (Psalm 51:10). On our own, we are too weak, fragile, and bent in our own way to become the people God created us to be. We might be able to reform some outward behaviors, but we will never be able to transform our hearts. The heart is the control room of our lives, and when we try to take control, we will only end up hurting ourselves and others (as David did). It is only when we surrender our hearts and our lives to Christ that God's renewing power brings us into new creation. Jesus declares, "I make all things new" (see Revelation 21:5). Among those "new things" are our hearts.

DEVOTION

Father, we thank you for your great love. We thank you that you have a plan and purpose for our existence. We submit to your work in our lives—expose the sin in our hearts, lead us to repentance, and help us to walk in your ways. We long to live in a way that is pleasing to you.

JOURNALING

What do you sense that God is revealing to you today about the condition of your heart?

_____

_____

_____

_____

_____

_____

_____

_____

_____

_____

_____

_____

_____

_____

_____

_____

_____

_____

_____

_____

_____

_____

FOR FURTHER READING

To complete the book of Psalms during this twelve-part study, read Psalms 139–150. For more Bible passages about being known by God, read Psalm 17:3–5; Proverbs 20:27; Isaiah 46:8–10; Jeremiah 1:4–5; 29:10–14; Matthew 7:21–23; John 10:25–30; Galatians 4:8–9; and Ephesians 2:8–10.

LEADER'S GUIDE FOR SMALL GROUPS

Thank you for your willingness to lead a group through *Life Lessons from Psalms*. The rewards of being a leader are different from those of participating, and we hope you find your own walk with Jesus deepened by this experience. During the twelve lessons in this study, you will guide your group through selected passages in Psalms and explore the key themes of the book. There are several elements in this leader's guide that will help you as you structure your study and reflection time, so be sure to follow along and take advantage of each one.

BEFORE YOU BEGIN

Before your first meeting, make sure the group members have their own copy of the *Life Lessons from Psalms* study guide so they can follow along and have their answers written out ahead of time. Alternately, you can hand out the guides at your first meeting and give the group some time to look over the material and ask any preliminary questions. Be sure to send a sheet around the room during that first meeting and have the members write down their name, phone number, and email address so you can keep in touch with them during the week.

There are several ways to structure the duration of the study. You can choose to cover each lesson individually for a total of twelve weeks of discussion, or you can combine two lessons together per week for a total of six weeks of discussion. You can also choose to have the group members read just the selected passages of Scripture given in each lesson, or they can cover the entire book of Psalms by reading the material listed in the "For Further Reading" section at the end of each lesson. The following table illustrates these options:

Twelve-Week Format

Week	Lessons Covered	Simplified Reading	Expanded Reading
1	The Path of Righteousness	Psalm 1:1–6	Psalms 1–14
2	Comfort and Rest	Psalm 23:1–6	Psalms 15–26
3	Confessing Our Sins	Psalm 32:1–11	Psalms 27–39
4	Relying on God's Strength	Psalm 46:1–11	Psalms 40–51
5	Confidence in God	Psalm 62:1–12	Psalms 52–64
6	Trusting in God's Goodness	Psalm 73:21–28	Psalms 65–76
7	Embracing God's Law	Psalm 89:19–37	Psalms 77–89
8	The Right Perspective	Psalm 90:1–12	Psalms 90–101
9	Getting Our Priorities Straight	Psalm 103:1–14	Psalms 102–114
10	God's Protection and Salvation	Psalms 125:1–126:6	Psalms 115–126
11	God's Blessings on Families	Psalm 127:1–5	Psalms 127–138
12	A Life of Purpose	Psalm 139:7–24	Psalms 139–150

Six-Week Format

Week	Lessons Covered	Simplified Reading	Expanded Reading
1	The Path of Righteousness / Comfort and Rest	Psalms 1:1–6; 23:1–6	Psalms 1–26
2	Confessing Our Sins / Relying on God's Strength	Psalms 32:1–11; 46:1–11	Psalms 27–51
3	Confidence in God / Trusting in God's Goodness	Psalms 62:1–12; 73:21–28	Psalms 52–76
4	Embracing God's Law / The Right Perspective	Psalms 89:19–37; 90:1–12	Psalms 77–101
5	Getting Our Priorities Straight / God's Protection and Salvation	Psalms 103:1–14; 125:1–126:6	Psalms 102–126
6	God's Blessings on Families / A Life of Purpose	Psalms 127:1–5; 139:7–24	Psalms 127–150

Generally, the ideal size you will want for the group is between eight to ten people, which ensures everyone will have enough time to participate in discussions. If you have more people, you might want to break up the main group into smaller subgroups. Encourage those who show up at the first meeting to commit to attending the duration of the study, as this will help the group members get to know each other, create stability for the group, and help you know how to prepare each week.

Each of the lessons begins with a brief reflection that highlights the theme you will be discussing that week. As you begin your group time, have the group members briefly respond to the opening question to get them thinking about the topic at hand. Some people may want to tell a long story in response to one of these questions, but the goal is to keep the answers brief. Ideally, you want everyone in the group to get a chance to answer, so try to keep the responses to just a few minutes. If you have more talkative group members, say up front that everyone needs to limit his or her answer to two minutes.

Give the group members a chance to answer, but tell them to feel free to pass if they wish. With the rest of the study, it's generally not a good idea to have everyone answer every question—a free-flowing discussion is more desirable. But with the opening reflection question, you can go around the circle. Encourage shy people to share, but don't force them.

Before your first meeting, let the group members know how the lessons are broken down. During your group discussion time the members will be drawing on the answers they wrote to the Exploration and Reaction sections, so encourage them to always complete these ahead of time. Also, invite them to bring any questions and insights they uncovered while reading to your next meeting, especially if they had a breakthrough moment or if they didn't understand something they read.

WEEKLY PREPARATION

As the leader, there are a few things you should do to prepare for each meeting:

- *Read through the lesson*. This will help you to become familiar with the content and know how to structure the discussion times.
- *Decide which questions you want to discuss*. Depending on how you structure your group time, you may not be able to cover every question. So select the questions ahead of time that you absolutely want the group to explore.
- *Be familiar with the questions you want to discuss*. When the group meets you'll be watching the clock, so you want to make sure you are familiar with the Bible study questions you have selected. You can then spend time in the passage again when the group meets. In this way, you'll ensure you have the passage more deeply in your mind than your group members.
- *Pray for your group*. Pray for your group members throughout the week and ask God to lead them as they study his Word.
- *Bring extra supplies to your meeting*. The members should bring their own pens for writing notes, but it's a good idea to have extras available for those who forget. You may also want to bring paper and additional Bibles.

Note that in many cases there will not be one "right" answer to the question. Answers will vary, especially when the group members are being asked to share their personal experiences.

STRUCTURING THE DISCUSSION TIME

You will need to determine with your group how long you want to meet each week so you can plan your time accordingly. Generally, most groups like to meet for either sixty minutes or ninety minutes, so you could use one of the following schedules:

Section	60 Minutes	90 Minutes
WELCOME (members arrive and get settled)	5 minutes	10 minutes
REFLECTION (discuss the opening question for the lesson)	10 minutes	15 minutes
DISCUSSION (discuss the Bible study questions in the Exploration and Reaction sections)	35 minutes	50 minutes
PRAYER/CLOSING (pray together as a group and dismiss)	10 minutes	15 minutes

As the group leader, it is up to you to keep track of the time and keep things moving along according to your schedule. You might want to set a timer for each segment so both you and the group members know when your time is up. (Note that there are some good phone apps for timers that play a gentle chime or other pleasant sound instead of a disruptive noise.) Don't feel pressured to cover every question you have selected if the group has a good discussion going. Again, it's not necessary to go around the circle and make everyone share.

Don't be concerned if the group members are silent or slow to share. People are often quiet when they are pulling together their ideas, and this might be a new experience for them. Just ask a question and let it hang in the air until someone shares. You can then say, "Thank you. What about others? What came to you when you reflected on the passage?"

GROUP DYNAMICS

Leading a group through *Life Lessons from Psalms* will prove to be highly rewarding both to you and your group members—but that doesn't mean you will not encounter any challenges along the way! Discussions can get off track. Group members may not be sensitive to the needs and ideas of others. Some might worry they will be expected to talk about matters that make them feel awkward. Others may express comments that result in disagreements. To help ease this strain on you and the group, consider the following ground rules:

- When someone raises a question or comment that is off the main topic, suggest you deal with it another time, or, if you feel led to go in that direction, let the group know you will be spending some time discussing it.
- If someone asks a question you don't know how to answer, admit it and move on. At your discretion, feel free to invite group members to comment on questions that call for personal experience.
- If you find one or two people are dominating the discussion time, direct a few questions to others in the group. Outside the main group time, ask the more dominating members to help you draw out the quieter ones. Work to make them a part of the solution instead of the problem.
- When a disagreement occurs, encourage the group members to process the matter in love. Encourage those on opposite sides to restate what they heard the other side say about the matter, and then invite each side to evaluate if that perception is accurate. Lead the group in examining other Scriptures related to the topic and look for common ground.

When any of these issues arise, encourage your group members to follow the words from the Bible: "Love one another" (John 13:34), "If it is possible, as far as it depends on you, live at peace with everyone" (Romans 12:18), and, "Be quick to listen, slow to speak and slow to become angry" (James 1:19).

Thank you again for taking the time to lead your group. May God reward your efforts and dedication and make your time together in this study fruitful for his kingdom.